KEEPING IN TOUCH

KEEPING IN TOUCH

F.C. Barrett's Newsletters
to Girton Servicemen and Women
from the Home Front
1943–1945

by

F.C. Barrett

Edited by
D.R. de Lacey

Illustrations prepared by
M. Parnwell

With members of the Girton History Group

F.C. Barrett M.B.E. 1910–1995

Copyright © 2001 Girton History Group
All rights reserved.
No part of this publication may be reproduced,
stored in a retrieval system, or transmitted,
in any form or by any means,
without the prior permission of the Editors.

ISBN 0-9539007-0-3

Typeset in Great Britain by
Aslan Ltd, Girton, Cambridge CB3 0QB
in 11/13 New Century Schoolbook
and printed by
University Printing Services, University Press, Cambridge

First published 2001

This publication was enabled by a grant from the
Millennium Festival 'Awards for All' scheme

Contents

Frontispiece: F.C. Barrett	iv
List of Illustrations	viii
Foreword	xii
Acknowledgements	xv
F.C. Barrett: An Appreciation by S. Robey	xvi
Map of Girton Village, 1938	xviii
The Letters	1
Appendix: Replies	156
Abbreviations	160
Index (prepared by Mr M. Tombs)	162

Illustrations

F.C. Barrett M.B.E. 1910–1995 (photograph courtesy Mrs S. Robey)	iv
Map of Girton Village, from the Ordnance Survey of 1938 (Crown Copyright)	xviii
An airgraph, typical of the many received by Freddy Barrett in reply to his letters (actual size approximately 4.75 × 3.75 inches, 120 × 95 mm) (photograph courtesy Mr W. Parnwell)	2
St Andrew's Church, Girton, before the removal of its railings for the War Effort, (probably c. 1925)	3
The old School, now used as a Village Hall and named in memory of Anna Maria Cotton (© Cambridgeshire Collection)	7
Ernie Wilson, R.A.S.C. (photograph courtesy Mr R. Lipscombe)	8
Girton Red Cross. Back Row: Mrs Hall, Gert Lyons, 'Jimmy' Naylor, Doris Naylor, Mrs Hancock, Heather Huddlestone, Honor Huddlestone, Mrs Lee, Mrs Johnson. Middle Row: Irene Nightingale, *unidentified*, Mrs Turner, *unidentified* Mrs Marshall. Front Row: Mrs Burgh, Rose Hancock (photograph courtesy Mr W. Parnwell)	10
Roy Ellis Beds & Herts Regt., Queen's Regt. 7th Armoured Div. (Desert Rats) (photograph courtesy Mr R. Lipscombe)	12
Len Hales, R.A.S.C. (photograph courtesy Mr L. Hales)	14
The Clock Tower, Girton (photograph courtesy Mr W. Parnwell)	21
L.A.C. Claude Kidman R.A.F. Wireless operator (photograph courtesy Mr R. Lipscombe)	23
Mrs Henrietta Wilfrida Leakey (photograph courtesy Manni Masons Photographic, ©MMP)	26
Cpl Les Impey, R.A.O.C. (photograph courtesy Mr R. Lipscombe)	29

Stan Dixon, R.A.F. pilot trainer and transport pilot (photograph courtesy Mr R. Lipscombe)	30
The Revd P.N.H. Palmer, former Rector of Girton, with his wife (photograph courtesy Mr R. Ellis)	32
Ron Lipscombe, R.N., D.E.M.S. (photograph courtesy Mr R. Lipscombe)	34
Girton School Centenary, January 1946. Pupils of the first Headmaster meet present-day children; the Revd L.G. Tucker top right (picture reproduced by kind permission of Cambridge Newspapers)	37
The Revd L.G. Tucker, Rector of Girton (picture reproduced by kind permission of Cambridge Newspapers)	38
Miss Mary Rudd, W.A.A.F. (photograph courtesy of her family)	41
Cadet Parade at Impington Village College, May 1943: British Official Photograph BC.6436, Crown Copyright reserved (picture reproduced by kind permission of Impington Village College)	43
Jack Balaam (photograph courtesy Mr J. Balaam)	45
Sgt Ken Mayes (Sgt Armourer) (photograph courtesy Mr R. Lipscombe)	49
A Steam Threshing Machine, part of the 'new' agriculture (© Cambridgeshire Collection)	50
The first Newsletter, March 1943	52
Miss Alice Hibbert-Ware (picture reproduced by kind permission of Cambridge Newspapers)	56
The Village Football Team including many of the recipients of this letter. Back Row: R. Evans, M. Ellis, S. Nightingale, B. Evans, E. Aero, W. Garner, *unidentified*, K. Naylor, B. Adams, R. Hankin, P. Gordon, D. Porter, T. Skinner, F.C. Barrett. Middle Row: N. Littlewood, J. Mansfield, R. Lipscombe, M. Pigden, P. Fletcher. Front Row: B. Hayles, *unidentified*, *unidentified*, *unidentified*, *unidentified*, *unidentified*, ? Catlin, *unidentified*, ? Catlin (photograph courtesy Mr W. Parnwell)	58

Post-War Council Houses in St Vincent's Way, Girton. (photograph courtesy Mr W. Parnwell)	63
Bob Coe, R.A. (photograph courtesy Mr R. Lipscombe)	66
The Old Rectory, at this time the home of Littleton House School (© Cambridgeshire Collection)	68
Salvage Cartoon (drawn by Margaret Parnwell)	72
Pte Tom Pauley, R.A.S.C. (photograph courtesy Mrs G. Allen)	74
Girton Follies, 1944: 'Salute the Soldier'. Back Row: Mrs B. Miller, Stanley Wheeler, Mrs R. Nightingale, Ruth Arthur, Albert Simmonds, Pamela Cornell, Mr. E. Miller, Robin Martlew, Raye Piggott, Mr. J.H. Ison. Middle Row: Jill Nightingale, Gillian Martlew, Shirley Brand, Eileen Pigden, Molly Foster, Maureen Taylor, Betty Skinner, Ernest Pigden, Mary Smith, Anne Tribe, Michael Wakelin. Front Row: Sylvia Tribe, John Miller, Anne White, Audrey Collison (photograph courtesy Mr L. Collings)	76
Girton Village Institute in 1944 (© Cambridgeshire Collection)	78
Cyril Wilson, Durham Light Infantry (photograph courtesy Mr R. Lipscombe)	80
Girton Home Guard with Mr Monkman holding the Shield won in a Battle Platoon Competition (photograph courtesy Mr Parr)	83
Duck End, Old Girton	86
The Alice Hibbert-Ware Memorial Garden today (photograph courtesy Mr W. Parnwell)	90
S/Sgt Tom Impey, R.E. (photograph courtesy Mr R. Lipscombe)	92
Steam Threshing in rural Cambridgeshire (© Cambridgeshire Collection)	94
A.Me. Jack Collings, R.N. (photograph courtesy Mr J. Collings)	98
Ken Deane, S.H.A.E.F.F. (photograph courtesy Mr R. Lipscombe)	100

Peter Thulbourne, R.A. (photograph courtesy Mr R. Lipscombe)	102
Girton Home Guard, on parade in the Village (photograph courtesy Mrs Y. Andrews)	109
Roland Wilson, Bevin Boy (photograph courtesy Mr R. Lipscombe)	115
Tom Evans, Bevin Boy (photograph courtesy Mr R. Lipscombe)	117
Corporal J. Hind, R.A.F. (photograph courtesy Mr R. Lipscombe)	121
The Baptist Chapel, spiritual home of Frank Dupont (© Cambridgeshire Collection)	123
Girton College, where students also helped to 'Dig for Victory' under the eye of Head Gardener Collings (photograph courtesy Mr L.Collings)	124
Harry J. Chapman, R.A.S.C. (photograph courtesy Mr R. Lipscombe)	127
George Betson, R.A.S.C. (photograph courtesy Mr G. Betson)	128
The present Girton Glebe School, opened in 1951 (photograph courtesy Mrs J. Harradine)	131
An Avro Lancaster, symbol to many of British air power (photograph courtesy Mr W. Parnwell)	137
Roy 'Gummy' Naylor R.N., R.M. (photograph courtesy Mrs P. Naylor)	141
The Women's Institute Hall, also used by the Home Guard as training H.Q. and rifle range (photograph courtesy Mr W. Parnwell)	145
A wartime Girton Village Cricket Team (photograph courtesy Mr M. Ellis)	147
Dick Evans, R.A. (photograph courtesy Mr R. Evans)	148
The War Memorial, Girton with (inset) the names of those who died in the Second War (photographs courtesy Mr W. Parnwell)	160

Foreword

In the dark days of 1943, an ordinary resident of a small Cambridgeshire village wrote a letter. It was a circular to some former members of his Village Youth Club now serving their country abroad. Freddie Barrett of Girton could hardly have realised then that he was beginning the production of an unique archive of military and local history. For two and a half years his cyclostyled monthly letters would catalogue the daily doings of his neighbours, and the snippets of news he received in reply from the Front, as he kept his boys in touch with each other and with the Village.

As the months passed the circle of recipients grew until it included all the Village's servicemen and women, and more people were drawn into writing for the letters. The letter for December 1944 gives a good sense of the numbers and diversity involved on both sides. Over 50 serving men and women are mentioned by name in this letter; 10 Villagers (ranging from a 5 year-old to the Chairman of the Parish Council) write a greeting note to be included with Mr Barrett's own.

The pleasure given by this correspondence may be gauged from this extract from one reply: 'I look forward to the news letters arriving very much and I still have every one that my father has forwarded to me and I often get them out and read them. I am the only one from our village in my battalion. I am sure you will be pleased to know that quite a number of my men read the NL and some have even wrote home asking for the same thing to be done in their own district'. Several of the replies suggested the publication of the collection when the War ended, but it has taken nearly sixty years for them to reach a wider public. Yet they remain as fresh and interesting as when they were first eagerly devoured by young men and women hungry for news of Home. Here are catalogued last weekend's football scores and the weather, together with the story of the fire which 'some mean person' put out before the Fire Brigade with its brand new engine was ready; as well as the greater issues of the day, Beveridge, the 1944 Education Act, and of course the momentous events of the closing stages of the War. Here we read the details of plans to develop a memorial garden to a local naturalist, by a community convinced that global conflict was a mere interruption in the even progress of their society.

The letters presented here are a chronicle of a village's life, not a scholarly journal. There were inevitable small errors and infelicities in the text; and from month to month Barrett's conventions changed. In order not to distract the reader we have chosen to correct obvious errors and create a greater uniformity of style. We may also enjoy a more attractive format than a typewriter allowed: underlinings in the original are represented here by italics. Annotations have been kept to a minimum: we have preferred for instance to expand the local abbreviations or obscurities rather than resorting to the scholarly ploy of footnotes. But as far as possible consistent with readability we have tried to provide an accurate transcription of the letters.

Our hope is that many people will enjoy the inherent interest of this chronicle, but to help those with specific interests we have provided an index. We have indexed all personal names, those events on which the letters have any significant content both in the war and on wider issues (politics, religion, education) plus certain local events and institutions which were important to Barrett and his readers. We also add expansions or brief explanations of abbreviations and terms which may be obscure to a contemporary reader.

Many of the recipients wrote back to Barrett, and he treasured the replies. What he considered the most significant of the content found its way back into the next month's letter, though for the local historian there are still many riches to be tapped there. The task of transcribing those letters would have been monumental and would have created an unwieldy project. In comparison, the task of editing an OCR transcript of the cyclostyled letters was straightforward enough to be manageable. However, the replies, and the originals of the Barrett letters, have now been lodged with the Cambridgeshire Collection and are available to serious students. For interest we have catalogued the replies in an appendix.

Before his death Mr Barrett bequeathed his collection of the letters and the replies to Mrs S. Robey, who has kindly also provided us with an appreciation. For the period of the correspondence (March 1943 – September 1945) there were four holes in this collection. It is clear that two months (September 1944 and August 1945) saw no letter written, and a copy of the March 1944 letter was subsequently located from another source. Thus only one letter remains lost, a remarkable fact for such an ephemeral archive.

For nearly a decade Girton residents have worked on the creation of an archive of our Village's history. The Girton History Group has its origins in Project 2000 which was set up in 1992 for the purposes of collecting Girton memorabilia and updating an earlier published history of the Village (*Girton: An Historical Survey*, ed H. Bashford and L. Bolgar, privately published in 1951). A considerable archive of material was collected before the project was abandoned. However, thanks largely to the efforts of two of its members, Bill and Margaret Parnwell, the Girton History Group was formed in March 2000 with its main objectives to publish selected material from this archive.

The collection of letters sent by the late Freddie Barrett to Girton Servicemen and Women between 1942 and 1945 was an ideal initial project. Under the Chairmanship of D.R. de Lacey, a Committee was established comprising M. Hornsey, S. Hornsey, H. Naylor, M. Parnwell, W. Parnwell, J. Scrine, R. Scrine and M. Tombs. A successful application to the Heritage Lottery Fund provided sufficient funds to produce this book and thus realised part of the original objectives of its predecessor Project 2000.

The original letters were automatically transcribed by Optical Character Recognition (OCR) on computer. Members of the Committee then undertook the laborious process of proof-reading and where necessary re-typing sections of the letters to provide the basic text. Dr D.R. de Lacey then edited the letters while Mrs M. Parnwell co-ordinated the photograph archive. Mr M. Tombs prepared the index.

An appeal through the Village Newsletter produced an additional wealth of photographs of Girton service personnel and other wartime photographic records: it is a matter of regret that we have not been able to include them all. We hope that what we have produced may stand as a tribute to all who served their nation from our Village.

The Editors
Remembrance Day 2001.

Acknowledgements

Many people have been involved in this project: it is a pleasure to acknowledge and thank them. From an early stage we had the help and encouragement of the Revd R Mackintosh and Mrs S Robey. The then Chairman of the Cambridgeshire Records Collection, Dr Peter Searby, and Dr E. Leedham-Green of the Cambridge University Library gave advice and encouragement. Dr Kate Perry of Girton College and Anne Thomson of Newnham College gave us access to their Archives.

Mr. George Boss (Curator, East Anglia Regiment, Imperial War Museum, Duxford) and members of the Northamptonshire Regiment Association; the Royal Engineers' Museum, the Royal Logistic Corps Museum and the Welch Regiment Museum helped in providing explanations for the abbreviations.

Mr R. Lipscombe provided invaluable assistance in locating and collecting photographs of Girton servicemen. We also wish to thank the following for providing photographs: The family of Mary Rudd; Mrs G. Allen; Mrs G. Andrews; Mr J. Balaam; Mr G. Betson; Mr K. Blunt; Mr H. Chapman; Mr W.J. Claydon; Mr R. Coe; Mr R. Cole; Mrs L. Collings; Mr J. Collings; Mr K. Deane; Mr S. Dixon; Mr W. Dixon; Mr R. Ellis; Mr M. Ellis; Mr R. Evans; Mr T. Evans; Mr L. Hales; Mr K. Hancock; Mrs J. Harradine; Mr J. Hind; Mr L. Impey; Mr T. Impey; Mr C. Kidman; Mr M. Lipscombe; Mr and Mrs K. Mayes; Mrs H. Mills; Mrs P. Naylor; Mr T. Nightingale; Mr W. Parnwell; Mrs R. Pauley; Mr S. Reader; Mr L. Smith; Mr P. Thulbourne; Messrs C., E. and R. Wilson. The Cambridgeshire Collection; Cambridge Newspapers; The Daily Telegraph and Manni Masons Photographic. The Warden and Librarian of Impington Village College for the archive picture of the College.

We have tried to contact all who have a copyright interest in materials published here. Our sincere apologies to any who feel we have infringed their rights.

The Millennium Festival 'Awards for All' scheme gave a generous grant to prepare and publish the text.

And finally we delightedly acknowledge the labours of F.C. Barrett, who envisaged, created and with foresight preserved for posterity this wonderful archive.

Freddie Barrett M.B.E. 1910–1995

Freddie Barrett thrust a bulging plastic bag into my hand. 'Newsletters about Girton I sent to our young people serving in the forces in the Second World War. I've always thought that there might be those interested in seeing them, but I don't know how to go about it. So I'm giving them to you; you'll know what to do.'

I didn't have the first idea, as it happens. But Freddie had entrusted them to me and something had to be done. And eventually it was, thanks to a dedicated team who realised their importance not only here in Girton but in the wider world beyond.

So, fifty-five years after the last of these thousands of words were written, this record of a village at war between 1943 and 1945 is published for all to see.

The word 'remarkable' is heavily over-used but in Freddie Barrett's case there really is nothing to put in its place. Born on the Isle of Arran, he came to Girton in the 1930's, with his wife and small son, and bought from a local farmer a piece of land at the top of Church Lane, being mindful of the advice he had been given that it was good to buy land near a church as monks always built on the best drained and most fertile soil in the area.

He worked for Dr Isherwood, a plant biochemist, at the Low Temperature Research Station in Cambridge on the Downing Street site as an experimental research assistant. In 1966 the section with which he was involved was moved to Norwich to become the Institute of Food Research. Thereafter, as a senior scientific officer, he commuted between Girton and Norwich until he retired, being awarded the M.B.E. in 1974 for his valuable contributions to food research.

For most men this would have been enough, but not for Freddie Barrett. For him there was also the world of sport in general and football in particular.

He was a member of the Council of the Cambridgeshire Football Association for more than thirty years, becoming a Life Vice-President and Chairman of the Policy and General Purposes Committee. For twenty-eight years he was Secretary to the Coaching, Youth, Selection and Schools Committee, and was also for many years the Association's representative to the Standing Conference of Sport. Among other offices which he held, Freddie was for eighteen years President of the Cambridge and District

Sunday Football League, and was a member of the Eastern Region Sports Council on which he was Vice-Chairman of the Participation Committee. He was also a founder member of the Committee of Management, and Director of the Kelsey Kerridge Sports Hall.

Freddie was not only a committee man but also actively involved in his beloved football both as a referee and a coach. He was a referee for fifteen years rapidly reaching Class 1 standard. Being Freddie, it is not surprising to learn that, at the end of the Second World War, he played a leading role in the re-establishment of the Cambridge Branch of the Referees Society, serving as President for six years. As for coaching, for thirty-two years he coached over a wide area and at all levels of the game.

And then there was Girton. There is no doubt about it, Girton United Football Club, of which he was President for forty-eight years, was very much at the top of his personal agenda. Before the 1939–45 war he was a goalkeeper, a committee member, and Chairman, whilst his coaching skills were for many years of great help to the Club, the all-conquering side of the mid-1950's bearing testament to his talents.

That, during the dark days of war, the thoughts of such a man should have turned to those to whom he had devoted so much of his time is in no way extraordinary. What is extraordinary, however, is that somehow, despite all else that he did, he found time to write these newsletters with their bits of gossip, their reflections on matters as diverse as the spring weather and the need to prepare a land fit for heroes for the returning servicemen to enjoy, fund-raising for the war effort and the layout of the Alice Hibbert-Ware garden. Thus he kept these young men and women in touch with their homes and families. In doing so, however, he also left the future an outstanding legacy.

At the end of this book you will find a list of all the service men and women who wrote thanking Freddie and passing on their news, which, in its turn, sometimes became part of the next newsletter. They too reach out to us from the past reminding of us of the sacrifices which were made that this village, and all the other communities in these islands, might continue to live in peace. So it is that, as we look forward to the new millennium, we salute with pride both the editor of the newsletters and his correspondents.

S.Robey.

xviii   KEEPING IN TOUCH

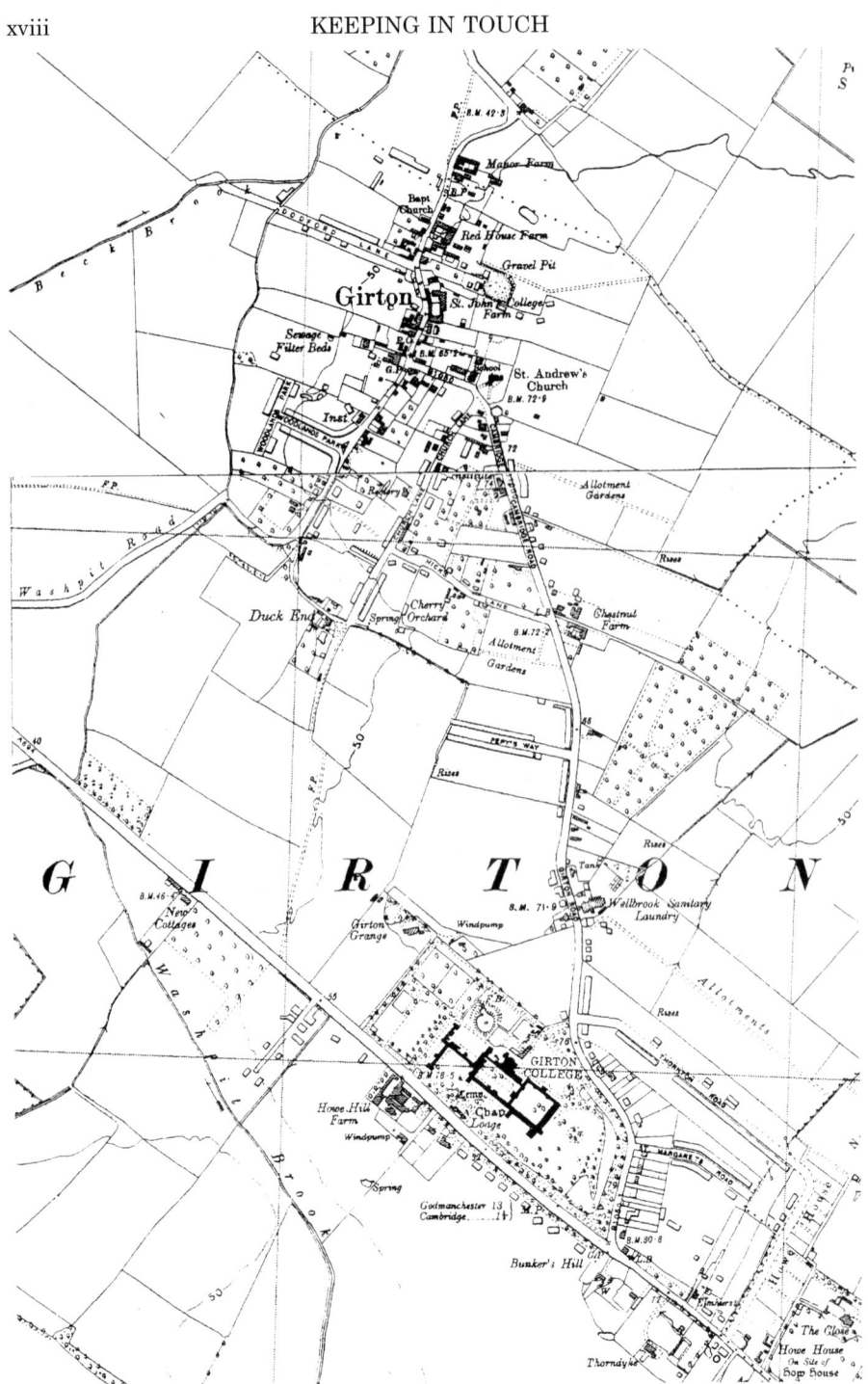

Girton Village (from the 1938 Ordnance Survey)

The Letters

6 Church Lane,
Girton.
March 1943

Dear

Since the outbreak of war an attempt has been made to keep in touch with our village boys serving in the forces. The evident appreciation of village news and friendly contact has developed the idea that we should together attempt a regular news-letter, which would provide a link between our village and those of its members absent on war service. A copy of this, our first issue, has been sent to each member of the Youth Centre and Young Men's Group at present serving. It is hoped that copies of future letters may be sent to anyone belonging to the village who is serving in the forces and who would care to receive one.

As a medium for village news of general interest, the success of our letter will obviously depend upon the measure of co-operation received from all interested in its circulation, and we shall appreciate personal news or general information that may be of interest to pass on each month. Also suggestions towards its improvement will be welcome at any time.

The Girton Youth Centre is still going strong, we get a good crowd each open evening and everyone seem to enjoy themselves. Last week K. Hancock and G. Blunt went as our representatives to Impington Village College to take part in the National Association of Boys' Club Leaders' Training weekend. I went over on Saturday and Sunday and they certainly seemed to be having a jolly good time. Did you know that the following members of the Youth Centre are now serving in the forces: C. Kidman, Ron Lipscombe, A. Evans, 'Midge' Ellis, R. Naylor and last to join G. Betson. Claude was home on embarkation leave last weekend. I was so sorry not to have seen him. We all send him our best wishes for a quick and safe return. During the same weekend Arthur and Midge were home on a 48hrs, they both looked well and they told me that they were enjoying Army life. We were highly amused to hear they share a double bed in camp, do you remember those boxing matches between them? Well, I guess there is some fun in that bed. Ron Lipscombe was home a week or so ago, he was about to be posted to a gunnery course before being detailed to a ship. 'Gummy' has arrived safely at his depot and according to his Aunt he has lost a couple of stones in weight – gosh! he must be having a rough time.

The football team has not been in action since before Xmas until today, they played Swavesey at home and Girton won 10–1. It was a strange team that took the field, many of the players were new to the village team, many of them were never heard of before. We did not see the game, but we are informed that Divers scored 6 of the goals.

As nearly all the members of the Young Men's Group are now serving in the forces its activities have been more or less discontinued but we are glad to receive letters occasionally from members scattered far and wide. News has come recently of Jack Collings, at present training for the Fleet Air Arm, Frank Dupont, Boyce and Ron Barber and Roy Nightingale. All in the R.A.F. are well and fit.

A very welcome airgraph recently arrived from Maurice Songer who has had a very strenuous spell as an R.A.F. Maintenance Mechanic in the Middle East. There has been no news for some time of Vic Riley, but we understand he is well and still 'this side'. We regret being unable to discover anything concerning John Nickel who disappeared at Singapore, but news is beginning to filter through and we hope soon to see his name in the list of prisoners of war.

We all heartily congratulate 'Stan Dixon, one of our seasoned air veterans of 22' who for his work on operations has been mentioned in despatches and promoted Flying Officer. Well done Stan!

[There is no signature]

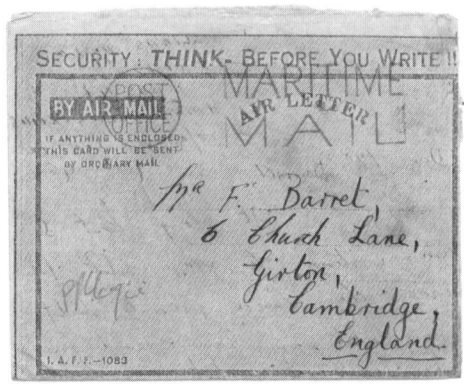

An airgraph, typical of the many received by Freddy Barrett in reply to his letters

6 Church Lane,
Girton.
April 1943

Dear

Since writing last month Spring has arrived officially and the village hedgerows and gardens are responding. Woody Green, Washpit Lane or Histon footpath again become inviting spots for an evening stroll, that is if one had the leisure to indulge, but the more serious business of 'digging for Victory' claims most of the village spare time just now. The allotments begin to show the value of a few hours well spent with spade and fork. If less picturesque than some other villages, to those whose roots are here Girton has an appeal of its own. To Girton men viewing the old village from such distances as the Libya Desert or the Hebrides, few spots are more attractive.

We are becoming quite used to seeing the churchyard without its railings and most of us have decided that, if useful, they were never an ornament. Perhaps one of our future united efforts may be to extend the old grey stone wall all round, bringing a more complete harmony into our village picture.

St Andrew's Church, Girton, before the removal of its railings for the War Effort

The Institute notice board this week carries the usual reminder that the Annual Parish Meeting will be held in the near future. No doubt we shall all turn out in strength, to listen, to approve perhaps even to criticise, the doings throughout the year of the elected representatives to our village parliament. The requirements of Civil Defence and the special needs of wartime are moulding us gradually into much more of a team than we ever were before, a team which we hope soon may be more complete by the addition of yourselves, ready for new tasks in a peacetime world. The mention of Civil Defence brings a reminder that the N.F.S. has been busy lately, making preparations for the new Headquarters, which is to be complete with Garage and sleeping accommodation. Static water is also to be made available for use in emergency. This is a different state of affairs to when at the beginning of the War the hose of the village brigade could not reach a water supply owing to its insufficient length! The local N.F.S. has been 'blooded', they attended a fire at Swavesey last month and a week or so ago they put out Farmer Coe's stack which was on fire.

During the month the Girton First-Aid Party may have been seen dashing about the Village followed by Party cars and ambulances. This activity was due to the fact that the Party were practising, in preparation for the County Competition. All First-Aid Parties throughout the county are to be examined in First-Aid and General Organisation. A cup will be presented to the most proficient on completion of the competition. It was Girton's turn on March 8th, and the party lead by Mr Dymond was sent to Oakington to deal with casualties from a bombed house, they extracted the 'victims', bandaged the 'injured' and sent the 'serious cases' to hospital. On the whole the party did extremely well and while there is no official announcement yet the examiners did express their admiration of the Girton Party.

Have any of our readers received a 2/6 postal order with a note conveying the compliments of the Entertainment Committee? Have you wondered where these 2/6's come from and who is responsible for its distribution? The Entertainment Committee is a sub-committee of the Trustees of the Village Institute. Last week they held their 3rd Annual meeting. Mr J.H. Garner was again elected chairman, at the same time high tribute was paid to him for his untiring efforts on behalf of the Committee. One of us, F.C.B., was elected vice-Chairman, Mr Lilley Secretary and 'Jim' Ison has been appointed organiser, he has been given a free hand to organise entertainments for and on behalf of the Committee. During the past two years proceeds from Concerts, Whist Drives, etc., has all gone to serving men and women and local children.

If a person is a prisoner of war they are not forgotten and at each distribution the value of a War Savings certificate is placed in a reserve fund on their behalf, which will be given to them on their welcome return to the village. The entertainments have been well supported and plans are now under way for a grand

'Wings for Victory' week 15th – 22nd May. Details of this week will be given in a later news-letter, but we can now say that there is going to be some form of entertainment every day during that week. Schemes are being put forward to urge the people to 'Save for Victory'.

Since our last letter the local football team with the aid of 'Foreigners' from Histon and Oakington have been fulfilling the remaining league fixtures. Hopes ran high for the League Championship and Cup when they defeated Swavesey 10–2 at home then Willingham away 5–3, and they received from Willingham without playing for them, two points for the home fixture. This left Saffron Walden and Girton both undefeated in the league, the home match with Saffron Walden you will remember was a draw. However the deciding match was held at Saffron Walden on March 20th, sad to say Girton were soundly defeated 9–0. On talking to the Girton players afterwards they agreed that the better team won although it was by no means the one-sided game the score leads one to believe. The final game of the season was a friendly with Histon Factory Home Guard at Histon, Girton won 6–2.

We are glad to hear that Ron Lipscombe has recovered from Yellow Jaundice, he tells us that he has missed his training, and consequently will be later joining a ship. Poor old 'Midge' Ellis has had a rough time, he has been in Hospital with an acute attack of Impetigo. We wish him a quick recovery.

During the past month, we have had the pleasure of seeing several serving men of Girton home on leave, among them were George Pauley, Sgt. Bob Coe, and Gummy, it is grand to see and talk to them and we wish they were amongst us again. We hope at any rate it won't be long before that happy day.

The first edition of the News-letter has brought several appreciative replies. If it is welcome at your end, don't forget we are equally glad to get yours.

Until next month,
Cheerio and good luck,
On behalf of the Village
Yours,
F.C. Barrett.
H. Bradfield.

6 Church Lane,
Girton.
May 1943

Dear

Easter has come and gone since last we wrote and following a short, but for most of us a very welcome break, life has again returned to its normal swing. A few visitors were to be seen in the village, and some of the boys were lucky enough to be on leave. Here and there one met evacuee youngsters, who, although now back in their own homes had accepted invitations to 'come for Easter'. There was no doubt about their pleasure at 'being asked'. Although probably most of us would agree that the evacuee problem, in all its aspects, could hardly be described as an unmixed 'blessing' it has undoubtedly taught us some things we needed to know about England's children, and has indeed inspired warm and kindly feelings in many hearts.

Occasionally in our letters we hope to include contributions from outstanding village personalities. This month it is Mr J.H. Garner, who certainly needs no introduction. His mention of the approaching big event in the history of the school will make a special appeal to us all and we think will also whet our appetites regarding the Girton School of the future.

The old School, now the Cotton Hall

Now here is Mr Garner's contribution:–
'I welcome and appreciate the opportunity afforded by our Village News Letter of sending you all a personal message. May we all at the School, Headmaster Staff and Scholars, send you at this Eastertide our heartiest greetings with a wish that Easter 1944 may see you all at home in Girton once more. Some of you who receive this letter are old Scholars of this School, some may have children in attendance; but all of you will be interested in the proposals now being considered for a new Education Bill. For years past, there has been a big demand for further Education of the youth of Britain and it does seem possible that this time definite steps forward will be made towards fitting our young people for their future careers with full education for all, up to eighteen years of age at least. However, I must not dwell on this aspect of the case. At the present time, a more intimate matter of great concern to Girton is the forthcoming centenary of your School. At the Parish meeting held on 31st March 1943 the Chairman drew attention to this fact and asked for any information which may be available as to the actual date of the school's foundation. Records available put it at about 1846; but there is certain evidence that the school existed before then. So if you have heard any "Grandfather's tales" of school days in Girton please send them along.

May I add one word about the Entertainment Committee, we have recently appointed a new one for this year and the members greatly appreciate the nice things you say in your letters about their efforts. We raised just over £122 last year and hope to better this in 1943.'

At the same Parish Meeting mentioned by Mr Garner the village was surprised to hear from the Leader of the First-Aid Party that he had received orders from the Powers-that-be that under a recent re-organisation scheme it had been decided to dissolve the Girton Party. This came as a shock and a blow to many people in the village for they had confidence in the Party which had been in existence since the outbreak of War. Several of the original members are still with us but others are scattered as far apart as the Hebrides and Palestine. We wonder if they recall the comradeship and happy hours spent sleeping in the tin hut or on siren duty? Do they recall those Xmas feasts when we decorated the hut, cooked our supper on the gas stove and toasted each other with Dale's bottled beer which tasted like champagne, again when one of our Party was called up how we wished him God speed and good luck? Never have I heard a cross word spoken and it is with real regret that the Party has to be split up before we have completed 'the Job', however if the authorities think they will thereby save man power and it is for the general good, 'so-be-it'.

Ernie Wilson, R.A.S.C.

Calm and unruffled as ever, Roy Nightingale was amongst those home for Easter. Having completed his special course and unfortunately also his leave, he has now returned with obvious pleasure to his old squadron. Jack Collings was also home recently, looking very fit and enthusiastic. Jack has made excellent progress in the strenuous training required for the Fleet Air Arm.

John Chapman writes with his usual cheery optimism from Cornwall. We have heard with real pleasure that Maurice Songer our R.A.F. veteran of Libya and Tunisia has been promoted Corporal. We were pleased to see in the village, Arthur Evans, Midge Ellis, G. Betson, Ron Lipscombe, 'Bill' Evans, E. Wilson, and as a stop press news, John Chapman is home.

This must be all until next month and don't forget those 'Grandfather's tales' for Mr Garner. What a pity our old friend the late Mr 'Tommy' Osbourn isn't still with us – his recollections would have been priceless.

Au revoir,
On behalf of the Village
Yours sincerely,
F.C. Barrett.
H. Bradfield.

6 Church Lane,
Girton.
June 1943

Dear

Owing to pressure of work the first week of June has gone before this month's letter is on its way. So far it looks as though 'dripping June, bringing all things in time', will more appropriately describe the weather than the proverbial 'flaming June' associated with cricket flannels and bees on overtime. The frequent showers are seen to good effect in the lush growth of the meadows, and haymaking has already begun. The War news since last month has proved quite a tonic and the village has shared the thrill that surged through the whole country when it became known that the enemy had been swept so dramatically from that vital 'Tunisian tip'. In keeping with most other places, a service of Thanksgiving and Remembrance was held on Sunday 16th May, and it was evident that the Village generally was fully conscious of the great issues at stake in the present conflict, of which the long drawn out battles from Alamein to Tunis and Bizerta had proved so vital a part! A platform had been arranged in the Churchyard, and from it, facing over the low stone wall to the Rec the Rev Tucker conducted the service. Lined up on the Rec were representative groups of the Home Guard and the various Civil Defence Services. Outstanding in the picture were the women of the village Red Cross Unit, smart and efficient, looking most attractive in their smart business-like uniforms.

The youthful voices of the choir boys led the singing of the old well-known hymns, in which all joined heartily. No doubt in thought and heart many were linked up with those absent from home.

A special tribute was paid to the Home Guard for their loyal and sometimes arduous service during the last three years. Following the service the various units gave practical demonstrations indicating that they had taken their training seriously and were ready for any emergency. When Sunday afternoon's respects and displays had been completed, the village was entertained in the evening to a concert given by the 'Choriton Trio'. So far as the village was concerned this was an innovation in the respect that children under 14 were not allowed to attend, it was for adults only. The children had already been provided for on the previous evening with a social

Girton Red Cross

and fancy dress dance. The concert was enjoyed in comfort by all, and there were many suggestions for more of a similar kind. Monday and Tuesday evenings were given over to a Whist drive and an exhibition of work done in and out of school by the children. It is noteworthy to mention that the children opened a Savings Bank at their display, and at it and during the week took £54 for Savings Stamps and certificates. On Wednesday evening the children gave a concert in the Men's Institute. The Hall was packed and quite a number of people were disappointed, as they could not gain admission. We hope to enlarge upon the subject of the Men's Institute in a future Newsletter, and ask your advice and co-operation as to how it could be improved when you return home.

On Thursday there was a Whist drive and on Friday the Youth Centre gave a concert, we think this concert deserves special mention. During the winter members of the Youth Centre under the direction of Miss Ellis have worked hard to produce two plays. The standard of acting was very good indeed and many people in the village were surprised at the ability of the young people. The week's activities concluded on Saturday evening with a grand dance, so ended a week in which much energy, thought and careful consideration was given to extracting money from people for savings in the most attractive and unobtrusive manner. It is invidious to mention names; but we feel that the name of 'Jim' Ison as organiser on behalf of the Entertainment Committee must be mentioned, he worked very hard indeed and it was due to his careful and thoughtful handling of the programme that the week went off so well.

Girton's Target was £6000; but we are proud to say that we attained the magnificent total of £9,200. The Entertainment Committee made a profit of £40 on the week's activities, this money will be used to provide prizes in the form of Savings Stamps for the Children's Sports to be held on the Recreation Ground on Whit Monday, and also to send you fellows a little extra.

We have been very busy attending to the business of winning the War; but we are not unmindful of the peace.

The Women's Institute have been discussing the future of elementary education, and the Beveridge Report. These discussions have been most interesting. On elementary education, most mothers desired a period of boarding school for their boys. On Beveridge they sent a resolution to our local M.P. stating that they accepted Beveridge in its entirety and were not prepared to have it whittled down. Finally the Girton Labour Party invited Prof. Harold Laski to explain Beveridge to the village. He was most interesting and witty, we must congratulate all concerned on such a successful meeting.

In our First News Letter we gave you an account of how we came to write the letter and the purpose behind it. May we restate that one of the purposes of the News Letter is to keep you in touch with your pals so you may know how they are getting on and also to provide you with Village news. We experience great difficulty in obtaining news of our serving men and women and would appreciate letters from you with news, which we could include in future News Letters. We also will be delighted to forward to you the address of anyone with whom you wish to correspond, whether in his Majesty's forces or not.

We have heard that our old friend Ron Lipscombe has left his training establishment and has been posted as a gunner to a Merchant ship, where he is we don't know; but if his shooting with a gun is as accurate as it was at goal his ship will come safely into harbour. Talking of the Navy, our latest recruit for that Service is Ron Cole. As he boarded the bus at the start of his journey to the recruiting base we wished him 'God speed' and a safe return. With him goes almost all the football team, there are one or two left, and they will soon be going; but we hope that they will get the job settled quickly and come home and reform their ranks on the recreation ground.

Roy Ellis of the Desert Rats

Arthur Evans manages to get home at the weekend, he has been parted from Roy Ellis who through being older than Arthur has been detailed for further training. Frank Dupont was home on leave from the Hebrides, and his almost next door neighbour on the Woodlands R. Huddlestone has arrived in Canada. Claude Kidman was last heard of in South Africa, Les Impey somewhere in the Middle East as also are our old friends Sid Gawthrop and E.J. Stearn. No wonder great things were done there for Girton always did breed men of valour! E. Wallis, brother of Miss Wallis who so kindly types this letter is in Palestine, so you see that Girton men are spread far and wide over the Globe.

It would be very interesting to get a bit of news from you for our next News Letter. What about that 'tough spot', or amusing experiences. Let us know how things are going?

On behalf of the Village,
Cheerio!
Yours,
F.C. Barrett.
H. Bradfield.

6 Church Lane,
Girton.
July 1943

Dear

July finds the village home front more or less as usual. The stir of 'Wings for Victory' week, described in some detail in our last letter, is being followed up by the normal 'Work for Victory' weeks which make up life at home nowadays. If perhaps less spectacular, these weeks are equally important. One of the outstanding things impressed on our minds during the War is the fact that most big events and important issues depend ultimately upon the 'spade work' which supports them. When we get, as most of us do occasionally, that 'fed up' feeling, this is a good thing to remember. It brings point and purpose even to those grey and less pleasant parts of army life and training.

On Whit Monday the Entertainments Committee organised sports for the Village children. The day was squally but it required much more than showers of rain to dampen the enthusiasm of the youngsters. In addition to races for the children there were races for Mothers and Fathers and a grand challenge race between a Service team of R.E.s, Searchlight Unit and the local lads. The R.E.s won the race, incidentally they were led by the champion long distance runner of N. Zealand, our local lads came in last amidst the cheers of the assembled company. At the conclusion of the day's sports Mrs Thompson on behalf of the Entertainments Committee presented the prizes to the winners in the form of Savings Stamps, so not only did they enjoy themselves but they also assisted the War effort.

We are glad to report that since last we wrote the relatives of our captured men in Singapore have received personal post cards which say they are fit and well. The first card came from Walter Dixon. His Mother was seen later that day and she was overjoyed. You can understand how she and the others must have felt when they knew that the long period of waiting and suspense was over. The other two wives to receive cards from their husbands were Mrs Austin of Woodlands Park and Mrs Ullyat of St Margaret's Road.

A few days ago the peace and quiet of the Village was disturbed by the clashing and clanging of fire engine bells. You all know Jack Gunn's little cottage on the corner of High Street opposite the old Post Office; for you who have been away for a long time the Post Office has changed hands, it is now in Mr North's cottage opposite the Women's Institute. Well, to continue, someone saw smoke and flames coming from Jack's house so they informed the Cambridge N.F.S. Almost immediately the Girton N.F.S. turned out and just as they were taking up position a fire engine and equipment arrived from Cambridge, a few moments later another engine arrived with further equipment, finally that 'Gorgeous' red engine complete with its telescopic ladder which will reach to the top of Cambridge's highest building arrived in state and prepared for battle. While all these engines and men were manoeuvring for position some mean person grabbed a stirrup pump and put the fire out! Slowly the engines turned round, the members of the brigade with a look of keen disappointment on their faces and no doubt a feeling of frustration returned to Cambridge.

The Women's Institute have recently formed a choir under the direction of Mr L.N. Tingey They competed with choirs from neighbouring villages at Impington Village College and were adjudged the best. A fortnight later there was a further competition which was held in St Andrew's Hall Cambridge; again Girton won and were highly commended for being the best Choir in the district. Our congratulations go to Mr Tingey and all concerned. We are given to understand that it is proposed to form a mixed Choir and that plans are afoot for a grand concert to be presented around Xmas time.

We have received a few letters from serving men and we thank you for them and we are glad to hear that you enjoy reading the News letter and wish it to continue.

Len Hales, R.A.S.C.

Many of you will be interested to hear that Len Hales, Carlos Griffiths and Claude Kidman are in India. Poor old Len scalded his leg and had to go to hospital, but the last Airgraph home stated that he has now recovered. He also stated that he and Claude had exchanged letters and hoped to meet each other in the near future. We also heard this week that Ron Lipscombe is at Colombo, Ceylon. He is fit and well and is enjoying the winter out there.

John McDougal in a recent letter mentions that he hopes to be home at the end of August. John has of late had a chance to see life from a new angle and time to think. He will return to us the better for his experience. He mentions he has been graded A.1. for the Army. Unless his ideas have changed he really fancies the Navy. Perhaps as a compromise he might get into the Marines! John is specially pleased to hear through the News Letter of Ron Lipscombe.

As a postscript to our letter this month we include a description of the Parish Council in Wartime by Mr Michael Pease, who is probably well known to most of us. About 23 years ago Mr Pease decided to settle in Girton, building a house in Reynold's Close, an old familiar Girton field name, which we are glad he has continued to use. Since then both he and Mrs Pease have closely identified themselves with the village life, working wholeheartedly for its development and progress and we owe them much. In addition to serving on various committees in the village, including the School Managers and Nursing Association, Mr Pease has also represented Girton in the wider sphere. Recently he gave a broadcast talk in the B.B.C. programme on his research work at Cambridge University. As Chairman of the Parish Council his capacity for impartial judgement combined with his firm and courteous handling of difficult situations has inspired the confidence of his fellow members. We felt you would like to hear from him how the Parish Council endeavours to represent the village interests in your absence.

Until next month Au-revoir and the best of luck on behalf of the Village.
Yours,
F.C. Barrett.
H. Bradfield.

POSTSCRIPT

As is well known, a Parish Council in peace time has very limited powers. It may spend money for public footpaths and recreation grounds and it may carry out certain delegated jobs such as scavenging and street lighting. It appoints the Parish School Manager (the Girton Parish Council appoints as well a manager of Impington Village College), and the Trustees of the Local Charities.

A Parish Council has however a very important duty to represent on all occasions the opinions and wishes of the local residents in all public matters and in this field there is in theory no limit to the matters which may be taken up, in practice one has to consider in each particular case whether the Parish Council's intervention is likely to do any good. In Girton the Parish Council has in recent years intervened effectively on Housing, Water supply, Sewerage, Impington Village College, the local Postal and Bus services and the Fire protection arrangements.

The War brought several new duties to the Parish Councils, in our case the most important ones being Salvage and A.R.P. The Parish Council is not a 'Scheme-Making Authority' under the Act; but it can spend out of the Parish rate to strengthen the local arrangements of the bigger Scheme of the County Council for the whole area. In Girton money has thus been spent in providing more comfortable quarters for the Warden's night post, in supplying additional equipment and medical stores at the First-Aid Post, and in organising a local Rescue Squad (which has now become merged with the Wardens' Service). But principally the Parish Council concerned itself from the beginning with coordinating in the Village the various A.R.P. services and in making known to the Village by means of printed Bulletins what to do in case of enemy raids. With this end in view the Chief Air Raid Warden has always attended the meetings of the Girton Parish Council. Happily we have had no Air Raid damage in the Village. In the matter of Salvage the Council has organised a collection of waste paper – the sale of this has brought in a handsome sum of money which has been used partly for helping good causes in the Village. The balance it is hoped will be a decent 'nest egg' for a village War Memorial and Victory Thanksgiving. Arrangements have also been made for salvaging metal, bones and rubber; but paper has been by far the most successful venture.

During the War there are no Parish Council elections – vacancies are filled by co-option. Mr Beaumont died just before the War, and his place was taken by Mr Elwood, and when the latter joined the R.A.F. Dr Walton accepted the invitation to fill the vacancy. Later Mrs Stewart, Mr C. Gawthrop and Mr W. Gordon (the last two members of very long standing) resigned and Mrs Turner (of Girton Corner), Mr Tingey and Mr Lawrence were co-opted.

M.S.P.

6 Church Lane,
Girton.
August 1943

Dear

This month's letter finds harvest in full swing and according to all accounts a jolly good harvest too. Five fairly big wheat stacks from 35 acres is a record on one farm in the village. Shortage of labour and a dry season this year have encouraged the use, on the bigger farms, of Combine Harvesters, which cut and thresh in one operation. Also quite an outstanding feature has been a revival of the old custom of gleaning and many villagers and townsfolk, spurred on by the prospect of corn without coupons, have turned out to clean up the stubbles.

August is a somewhat quiet month in the Village, as most folks are either helping in the harvest or are away on holiday; but the children come to the fore during this month of holidays. We see very little of the older boys and girls during term time as they are engaged all day at our Village College at Impington. So the holidays bring the chance of renewing touch with them. This was done fully on Bank holiday when a festival was arranged for them by the Entertainments Committee. Mr Ison was Master of Ceremonies and organised a procession of decorated bicycles and prams on the Recreation Ground. The results were most spirited and amusing! War Slogans were well represented, e.g. 'Save your Salvage and help to win the War', 'Dig for Victory', 'Don't be a Squander Bug'. The Committee had the good fortune to procure the help of Miss Butler, Mistress of Girton College, to judge of the best decorated vehicles. It was no easy job, but when completed the winners were presented with saving stamps. A huge source of joy to the youngsters were the two beautiful Shetland ponies on which rides round the Rec could be had at a penny apiece. This brought the children's part of the festivities to a close; but the adults continued with a dance in the Men's Institute, the profits from which amounted to approximately £9.

An outdoor religious Service was held on the Rec on Sunday July 25th. It was arranged by Mr Haw of Thornton Road. The Histon Salvation Army band provided rousing musical accompaniment. The choral section of the Women's Institute sang 'Jerusalem' by Blake, 'Thanksgiving', and 'England, Arise' words by Edward Carpenter and music by Leonard Tingey who also conducted all three songs.

The deep sympathy of the village residents has been with Mrs Pease in the recent loss of her Father, Lord Wedgwood. He was a great personality and an ardent worker for the Cause of Freedom.

We have had much pleasure in hearing from a number of serving men during the past month. The greatest surprise came with the appearance of our old friend Sid (Ginger) Gawthrop. We all thought he was in N. Africa with the Tank Corps but a week ago he appeared at 6.30 a.m. in Church Lane. We were asking his father about him and this was his description of what happened. 'The previous night my wife and I were discussing why we hadn't received a letter from Sid. We thought of all sorts of reasons until we fell asleep. The next morning I got up to cook my breakfast before going to work, I had just broken an egg in the pan when I heard a voice shouting "Anyone about!" I looked at my egg, turned it over and thought "I know the sound of that voice, but I must be dreaming" so I shook myself, rubbed my eyes, gave the egg a prod and again the voice shouted, "Anyone about!" I knew that I was awake for there in front of me stood Sid. I shouted to Mother and Sid's wife and I'll leave you to imagine the rejoicings'. Well here is the reason for Sid's return to England for 28 days leave. Out in N. Africa, as you all know, they have been capturing a number of Italian prisoners lately and so it came about that they collected a boat load which had to be shipped to England. Naturally a guard was required for them, so it was decided that the guard should be picked from men who had had a child born to them since they had left home and special hardship cases. Sid qualified in the former category and so he has been able to see his family and we are sure you all wish him a happy leave and a safe return trip.

We have heard from the Cranfield brothers Tony and Harry. Tony is on a battleship in the Mediterranean and has been allowed by Censor to say that his ship has taken part in recent happenings there. In a previous News Letter we mentioned that Girton men were on land and that was the reason for the fight going go well! Now we've got a naval man in the fight, so why worry!

In a long letter from Harry he recalls happy days in Girton and says how much he appreciates the News Letters and the news of Village lads. He was in hospital with cartilage trouble when he wrote; but by now we hope he is well again. You all know that

Harry was amongst the first to join up from the Village, he served in the Norwegian Campaign in 1940, so can be counted as one of our 'Veterans'. Ron Barber writes from N. Ireland to say that he looks forward to the News Letter and is disappointed when it is late.

Roy (Gummy) Naylor also writes a cheery letter, he mentions that he is going through a Signals course. Whilst there he met Ron Cole and they spent a happy fortnight together before Ron was drafted to M.T.B.s elsewhere. Roy has since been home on leave, he really does look fine. We are sure that he has grown three inches taller and quite a lot broader. George Betson, Arthur Evans, Robert Burrows, Bob Coe and Ron Barber have been home on leave, it's nice to see them again, we wished that you lads in distant parts could come.

Cyril (Son) Wilson in a recent Airgraph home says he had been in the front line (India) and had just returned to base. Carlos Griffiths was in hospital, also in India. Stan Dixon has arrived in Canada in order to train as a Pilot, he has been an observer since the outbreak of War and has flown thousands of miles but as he said 'I've always wanted to fly the kite myself'.

Mr L. Burgess, who will be remembered for his good work in organizing the early activities of the Young Men's Club, was home on leave recently. Looking extremely fit and well he is now serving as Leading Aircraftman in R.A.F. Signals. Boyce Barber has moved nearer home, to Long Melford. Roy Nightingale, still 'well down to it' on the maintenance of R.A.F. Bombers, was home on leave recently.

It is interesting to hear of all the adventures of our lads and it occurred to us that it would be a good idea if at the end of the War we collected together the Names, Regiments etc. of every serving man and woman from Girton, together with a short account of their adventures and published them in book form together with an account of all that has been done at home by such bodies as the Entertainment Committee etc., so that all may have a permanent record. Do you think this a good idea? If so write and let us know and start writing down details.

Our postscript this month is by Mr Sterndale Burrows of White Gate, whose interesting talks will be recalled by earlier members of the Young Men's Group. Long resident in Girton, Mr Burrows has for many years practised as a Solicitor in Cambridge. For the last quarter of a century he has held the position of Clerk of the Peace to the Borough of Cambridge, having previously been Deputy Clerk for 18 years, a record surely unique in local history. As an Undergraduate he stroked the third May boat for Trinity Hall in 1896 and did good work as a Youth Leader at Christ Church and the Albert Institute. A keen Churchman, with an intimate knowledge of Church affairs, he is deeply concerned as to the place of Christian thought and teaching in the post-war world

The increasing interest by the village generally in the News Letter is very encouraging. It can only be at its best when it expresses the wishes and feelings of us all, so once again a reminder that your news and ideas are always welcome.

Until next month Cheerio and best wishes, on behalf of the Village.
Yours,
F.C. Barrett
H. Bradfield.

POSTSCRIPT

The Church Tower,
Girton.

I am waiting and watching, with my face ever towards the Road – the road along which you will return. I may not be the first to see you, but I shall see you as you come swinging down the road – home to those who are also waiting and watching – wives, mothers, brothers and sisters, aye and fathers too, who say so little while they think so much, and little lads and maidens who will welcome you as never before. Maybe you will see the little people grown after these years of absence, but they will be the same to you as ever they were and dearer too for the joy of being reunited. As I look out upon the scene around me I mark the seasons as they pass – half of the year have I ticked off and chimed the quarters and the hours and now the harvest is here. Soon I shall hear beneath me the hymns of Harvest, and Autumn will herald the wintry days to come when wind, rain and snow will splash my face and make my hands heavy. Still I shall wait and watch with my face ever towards the road – the road of your return. There is much to see from where I am placed. I watch the Rooks come home at evening time. They seem to have changed their quarters or abandoned their old home in the Madingley woods, for now I see them more often pass me northwards battling with the wind, heavy no doubt with crops full of wireworms. Their job for the day is done, and like the little birds whose homes are here they seek their rest, and then the darkness falls and the night becomes quiet save for the gentle breeze that rustles the great trees around me. One by one the stars come out, the last rays of the sunset fade and die; the last cyclist rides home and I am left to wait alone and watch with my face ever towards the road. The little grey bus will trundle up in the morning and turn with its bonnet towards the road, and when I give the signal will start for the Town again with its load of workers. Some with shopping baskets empty, to come back full, others with their equipment for the day's work, all full of hope and faith that peace is not far off. Then, be it term time, come the boys and girls to school. I hear their happy chatter in the playground and on the Recreation Ground, and once more the world gets busy again.

The Clock Tower, Girton

Overhead a Bomber drones away on some mission or perhaps a practice flight, and Spitfires or Hurricanes flash by on some important errand. Back comes the little bus from hour to hour with its shopping baskets full, and so the day wears on while I keep watching with my face ever towards the road, till the night comes again – night with her mighty train of stars, the blazing beacons of an ordered Universe, reminders, dare I think, of Eternity in which I am but a time keeper. Thus I wait and watch with my face ever towards the old road – the road you know so well – the road which you can see in your mind's eye and long to tread again. I am, as I think you will have guessed, your old friend the clock on the Church Tower of Girton.

6 Church Lane,
Girton.
September 1943

Dear

It is with regret that I have to open this month's letter with the news that Mr Bradfield, part author of the News Letter, has through overwork become ill. He has been ordered by his Doctor to rest, to give up all work for the next three months and even then to do only that which is essential. He was at the theatre – the first time he had allowed himself to relax for a long time – when he was suddenly taken ill. I am sure you all join in wishing him a speedy recovery. I personally shall greatly miss his assistance with the News Letter, it was wholehearted and always helpful.

When we wrote to you a month ago who would have been so bold to predict all the events that have taken place? The capitulation of Italy, the surrender of her Fleet at Alexandria, the landing and advance on the Italian mainland by our 5th and 8th armies! When the capitulation was announced over the B.B.C. the news spread with lightning rapidity and everyone was suddenly smiling and saying 'Have you heard'? There was a quiet satisfaction everywhere but no outward manifestation of rejoicing of the flag waving kind, one rather got the impression that a bridge had been crossed but that more and important work lay ahead, and so the time for rejoicing was not yet.

The Girton Parish Council had assembled for their monthly meeting when the capitulation was announced and I am glad to tell you that they expressed the feelings of the village by sending a telegram of congratulations to the Prime Minister.

On the following Saturday a grand Victory Parade was held in Cambridge, but again there was an air of 'Too early to shout Victory, let's get back to work and finish the job!'

Talking of military matters, you will be interested to hear that the Home Guard Company of which Girton is a part, have been presented with a sword of Honour. As far as I can gather it was an inter-company competition; each Platoon was examined as to their efficiency. Girton's part was to demonstrate 'Turn Out' Defence and tactical fieldcraft. They carried out their tasks under Lt. Monkman's instructions with such efficiency, and the examining officer was so impressed, that he gave to the Girton Platoon the five extra marks which could be presented to the best Platoon of any company. Girton were fourteen marks ahead of any other platoon, and so greatly assisted their company to win the sword of Honour.

It is interesting to hear how our serving men are getting on in other countries. The following is an account of how P/O Hall of St John's Farm was received in Canada. For many years the Halls lived in King's Lynn a place name known to Canadians, so P/O Hall was given a great welcome. The Vancouver Herald, just received in Girton, records that he arrived there on a short leave from the prairie where he is training young airmen. P/O Hall, states the journal, 'comes from King's Lynn, Norfolk, England the birthplace of Captain George Vancouver. Upon reaching Vancouver P/O Hall visited the City Archives where he was told about the New King's Lynn named after his old town. Later in the day he attended a meeting of the Council and was introduced to the gathering, as he rose to acknowledge the welcome he was loudly cheered'.

During the past month we have received letters and airgraphs from various parts of the globe, all the writers express their enjoyment at receiving the News Letter and hearing about 'Dear old Girton'. A long letter from Claude Kidman, who is now in India. He gave an account of his journey out to that country. The following is an extract from his letter. 'The trip was uneventful all the way out, we stayed in South Africa four weeks. I had a very good time there, just imagine spending a few weeks in a troopship and then being "let loose" amongst every type of fruit one can think of, well you can guess what happened. I just "scoffed and scoffed" bananas, oranges, grapes etc., etc., but I suffered after!'

L.A.C. Claude Kidman R.A.F.

Well, Claude, I should think it was worth it. I should have loved to have been with you and shared your pain!

I also had a long and interesting letter from E.J. Stearn, you will all remember him. His house is opposite Mr Garner's, close to the Church and School; incidentally he is now a Staff-sergeant. He had many interesting things to say, first that he had spent many happy hours with Tom Pauley and was glad to report that Tom was very well, that they often talked about Girton, 'the shade of the trees over the Blacksmith's shop, the chiming of the Church clock and the shouts of the children at play on the Rec.' These were happy memories recalled amongst the vast wastes of sand and the sight of the occasional camel. He also met another Girtonian, – I believe I have mentioned it before – Basil Wallis, brother of Miss Wallis who still so kindly types this letter. Mr Stearn was on a visit to the Great Pyramids when by chance he spoke to Basil. Basil is an M.P. in the R.A.F. The second point made by Mr Stearn, let me quote his exact words 'The New Educational Bill may bear much fruit for our children, much is going to fall on their shoulders eventually, in rebuilding from the chaos which will remain after this struggle is over'. Now I feel that is a most important statement and I should like to devote a whole News Letter to it. There are so many aspects of the case which require discussion and clear thinking, and I am sure many people are alive to the opportunities now confronting. At the same time it is up to us, and when I say 'us' I mean ourselves personally. It is a job far too important to leave to the 'other fellows' and we have got to fight for better education with equal, if not greater, energy than we now use against the enemy. We must decide on what lines we have to build our new educational system.

Are we going to amend the old, or shall we have to use all our thinking powers to a resetting of our sense of justice and values. It is by clear thinking that we can control the course of things, of our human nature, civilisation and all else. It is a tragedy that in this 20th century, nearly all people gladly suffer, work and slave and pay fabulous sums of money for destruction, why cannot we do the same for constructive work in peace time? We must never for a moment 'let up', and when you return you must join and make a solid front in the fight, remember always, 'the price of freedom is eternal vigilance'.

The Girton Youth Centre which re-opens on Tuesday next, has invited Councillor Hardman, M.A. Ll.D. who is chairman of the County Youth Clubs Associations to come and address the village on 'Education in Britain after the War'. We hope everyone in the village will come and hear him. I hope to give you a report of the meeting at a later date. The above lecture is but one of the many activities which has been planned by members of the Centre for their coming sessions. There are to be monthly educational films and discussions. There will be time for handicrafts, Drama and the usual recreational activities and we hope for a canteen.

Some kind person, who wishes to remain anonymous, has offered a prize of 10/6 for the best essay entitled, 'How can we improve the Village?' The competition is open to our members serving in the forces as well as those at home. The closing date is December 15th – sufficient time to make the prize a Xmas present for the winner. We should appreciate essays on this subject from all of you who have seen other villages in this and other countries, your accumulated ideas will be invaluable.

You will have read, I hope with interest, the postscripts which have been attached to the News Letters. I now wish to ask you for contributions for the Postscript. Please use the News Letter to greet your pals and to express thoughts and ideas, both practical and theoretical.

The Postscript this month is written by Mrs H.W. Leakey, who is a graduate of Newnham, she has lived at The Close, Girton for the past 11 years. Mrs Leakey herself says, 'her life is one of inglorious trifles'. The following are some of her official positions in the Village: President of the Women's Institute, Organiser of the Child Welfare Centre, Chairman of the Youth Centre Adult Committee. A Trustee of the Village Institute, Assistant Billeting Officer, Organiser of the Emergency Food Supply and at the moment on two days per week she is teaching handicrafts to wounded soldiers in hospital at Cambridge. I believe what Mrs Leakey would most like is to be thought as a friend of the Village.

Until next month cheerio and best wishes, on behalf of the Village.
Yours,
F.C. Barrett.

POSTSCRIPT

The Close,
Girton.

My mind shrank when Mr Barrett asked me to write for this letter. Then suddenly I realised that it is to the father of Ann who so loves her orange juice, to the Uncle of Christopher who still shouts when we weigh him, to the elder brothers of our present Youth Centre and to the husband of the friend with whom I collect rose hips full of Vitamin C. So I'm not going to write solemnly after all; but am just going to gossip about the things that are growing in Girton.

Well the vegetables grow and one meets people pushing handcarts full of carrots, onions, and potatoes home from their allotments. The hamperful of fresh vegetables still goes to the Minesweepers every fortnight from the village, and the Women's Institute members are again going to send a great sack of onions to an onionless north country village – very special onions this year, grown from seed sent as a present from Institutes in Canada. Oh and the apple crop! I wish you could see it. The Newtons are shining scarlet and the Cox's are not just in proud singletons, but in great greenous clusters.

And the Village May tree grows, and oh how the village babies grow. Every Welfare day we give out about 80 bottles of Government orange juice, and if you can believe it the Medical Department wrote me a solemn letter asking why our babies seem to prefer orange juice to codliver oil!

Mr Watson's hair cutting room seems to grow fuller and fuller, so I suppose Girton hair grows too, makes perchance a hair cut in that little and friendly room just an excuse for the shocking male habit of gossiping. And now in the village it grows dusk at 7, so mercifully we can no longer work out of doors till 10 and 11. Think of us pulling our Black-out curtains and as we sit and sew or work we think of you. And hope shall grow, and friendliness shall grow, and a great determination to have a better and fairer England shall grow and grow, and grow.

H.W. Leakey

Mrs H.W. Leakey

[The letter for October 1943, if written, is missing]

6 Church Lane,
Girton.
November 1943

Dear

Since last I wrote to you, autumn has altered the face of our Village. Let us suppose that you in distant lands could catch a 102 Bus from the Town to Girton Corner and then walk to the Village. What would you now see? On alighting from the Bus the glorious colours in the coppice which surrounds Girton College. The horse chestnuts which were a mass of gold a week ago are now nearly bare and all their blood red leaves lie on the road; the palm of beauty goes to the Golden Maple and the guelder rose which is a deep reddish purple. Opposite St Margaret's Road are some stately beeches, the tops are edged with red and gold. These promise even richer colours at the end of the month. A little further on you would see in quite a number of gardens the Sumach tree with its red candles and crimson leaves. After passing the north entrance of Thornton Way, you reach the Laundry and opposite and behind 'Culdrien' is a large field, the sight of that field this week has brought back to me memories of the last war. In it has grown a crop of potatoes, and our older children, those who attend Impington Village College, have helped with the lifting of the crop. The weather – if I'm allowed to mention it – has been fine and warm, but in spite of this, some children to whom I have spoken have complained of backache and feeling tired. I can vividly recall how in the last war I too assisted a farmer in Scotland to lift his potatoes, and to this day I can still see and feel my chapped and swollen fingers as I struggled in the wet and mud. Each time I have passed the Girton field, and I pass it not less than four times a day, the thought has come to me 'Will the wheel of fate again turn a full cycle so that our grandchildren will have to lift potatoes in the next War?' I hope not, can we now say 'they shall not'?

Continuing our home coming we pass the allotments with their array of 'winter greens', clamps of potatoes with wisps of straw sticking out the top, derelict onion beds, and a few ardent gardeners already doing their winter digging. Passing Hicks Lane we come to the Village Institute, and as we approach it we can read the notices on the board outside. These announce a Whist drive on Thursday, a Dance on Saturday and on Sunday evening a grand concert to be given by the Corynton Trio. If we draw closer and look at the bills we shall see at the foot of each the statement 'In aid of Members of the Village serving in H.M. Forces'.

The Entertainments Committee held a meeting last week to decide upon their winter programme. They also decided upon something else, I shall not mention it, but I hope you will see the result of the decision in the near future. Talking about the Entertainments Committee, I have told you about its various officers, but completely failed to tell you that all the donations are despatched, and records are kept, by Mrs Thompson and Mrs Wilderspin. These two ladies work very hard indeed and I was glad to be able to convey to them and the rest of the Committee your grateful appreciation for all they are doing. Leaving the Institute we arrive at the Church where already the harvest hymns have been sung, and where the limes which surround the Church are already shedding their leaves after the first early frosts. Have you ever noticed that on November 11th when we stand with bowed heads for the two minutes' silence, only a leaf or two will rustle in the breeze?

I have made several calls upon Mr Bradfield during the past month, and I am glad to report that each time I have seen him I have noted with pleasure his continued improvement. The last time I called he was gently pottering about in his greenhouse and he told me that already he felt like a new man. He expressed a desire to write a postscript for the News Letter when he feels up to it, I am sure you will all look forward to reading it at the earliest opportunity, not only for his subject matter, but because it will be an indication to us that he has recovered.

May I add a further note with reference to the proposed essay on 'How I can improve the Village?' You will remember the competition is open to members of the Youth Centre. The donor of the prize has agreed to my suggestion that the prize be awarded for ideas rather than good English, he has also expressed a desire to award a book token to the value of 10/6 rather than the actual money, although he will not make this a condition of the award.

During the past month I have received from serving men quite a number of interesting letters. I have also gathered information, and your messages from your wives, parents and sweethearts. A long and interesting letter came from Cpl. Len Hales. He says 'It is almost two years since I left England to do my duty, during this time I have spent some of it in Africa and Egypt, finally arriving here in India. It seems like a life time having travelled so many thousands of miles, seen so many places and had so much excitement that it hardly seems possible that so much could be crowded into so short a time'. Len continues, 'The more I see of this country the more I realise there is no place like home, there are a few advantages here such as fruit, eggs and cigarettes, but nothing compared to that obtaining at home'. In closing he says how much he enjoys the News Letter and wishes to convey his greetings to all his pals, especially to Les Impey who was his colleague.

Strange as it may seem I received almost by the next post a letter from Les Impey who is in N. Africa, in his letter he wishes to send greetings to Len and his parents. He says 'he is fit and well and quite inured to the heat'. He finds it most interesting to see the grape vines, and how the Arabs pitch the grapes into carts and carry them away to be pulped and turned into an amazing variety of wines, which, he says 'are very potent'. Finally he sends best wishes to the News Letter – may it continue – I look forward eagerly to receiving it.

Les Impey, R.A.O.C.

A letter just received comes from Frank Dupont, who is somewhere in the western isles off Scotland. He hopes for the rapid recovery of Mr Bradfield, and I am sure, will be interested in the news we now send of him. I was amused with an incident which Frank mentioned. It is as follows. There was to be a special service in English at the little Church of Scotland, a 'liberty run' was arranged with the truck. After much excitement 13 airmen with polished buttons and clean shining faces arrived at the Church. Soon they found that a mistake had been made and the service was in Gaelic as usual! At the service the people stand during prayers and sit to sing psalms, no hymns and no musical accompaniment to help the psalms down.

KEEPING IN TOUCH

A postcard from Stan Dixon informs us that he is spending a well-earned leave at Niagara Falls, Canada – he'll soon have to go to Mars for fresh scenery!

John Chapman, who is with Heavy Ack Ack somewhere on the south coast, in a letter to Mr Bradfield, says he was in recent exercises off the French coast. John experiences difficulty, I suppose it is common to all of you, that of obtaining a hot bath. The Y.M.C.A. solve John's difficulty by coming round to his site with a mobile bath so they can really clean up. Since John wrote he has been home on a 48 hrs. This coincided with his 21st birthday. Congratulations John, accept all our good wishes.

Stan Dixon, R.A.F.

In a recent letter Boyce Barber is concerned about Mr Bradfield, he is also concerned about whether he will have outgrown his ancient friend his feather bed when he returns home, he has found that he can sleep so very comfortably on any floor. Maybe the solution to the problem would be to lie on the floor and wrap himself up in the carpet! Well, I suppose he will be no different to all you other chaps, you'll have no complaints that the feathers are hard when you really have the chance to lie on them.

John McDougal seems to be getting along well with life in the army, somewhere in Northern Ireland, he thoroughly enjoys the P.T. and sporting side, but suggests that we ought not to join for the fun of being a soldier. He entered for the company sports the other day, in addition to winning a race by 3 seconds he also won 5/– offered by his commanding officer. Well done John, best of luck for future ventures.

Finally I hear that Jack Collings has arrived in America. When he arrived he said his eyes nearly popped out of his head when he saw oranges, bananas, Nestle's milk chocolate and real ice cream in the shops! He rushed in, bought some of each, including a large cornet and sat down and ate them up one by one, his only regret was that he could not share them with his folks at home.

Very little has happened in the Village since last I wrote. Some of you will be interested to hear that Miss Hazel King was married last Saturday to Cpl. Harrington. The ceremony was solemnised at the R.C. Church, Cambridge and a reception was held at the Village Institute.

The postscript this month is written by a very old friend of Girton 'Mr' Palmer. He requires no introduction to Girton people, but there may be a few readers who have joined our ranks since he left. 'Mr' Palmer was rector of Girton 1930–37, during that time he and his family endeared themselves to everybody in the village. Keenly interested in young people he would help them in all their difficulties. I know of several instances where a young person would await him after morning service with the query, 'Can you help me with my algebra?' or yet another, 'Can you help me with my Latin verbs?' The answer was 'Of course, yes'. Can you think of a better way of endearing yourself to the young? Again, Mr Palmer was a great sportsman, he was interested in all ball games, but I think that cricket was his first love. The game to which he refers was played on the Magdalene ground in the final of the Milton and District Cup between Girton and Eversden. Girton batted first and made a good score – Mr Palmer himself contributing 50 runs. Eversden's turn came to bat, their score mounted gradually until it got dangerously near to Girton's. Cecil Cole, Captain of the Girton side, held a consultation on the field, all sorts of suggestions were made but no one thought of Mr Palmer as a bowler. However, as the men took up their respective positions to continue the game, Cecil called over Mr Palmer and asked him to bowl, at the same tine, a remark was heard on the field 'That's done it, we've lost the match'. Not a bit of it, Mr Palmer with his slow swinging bowling soon had the batsman in trouble, the first was caught at the wicket. In the pavilion that batsman frightened all the others by telling them that he had never seen bowling like that, before. In a very short time Eversden were out and Girton won the cup, how many times the cup was filled that night in the 'local' is quite another matter.

That will be all the news for this month, many thanks for your letters, keep on writing, I am always glad to know how and where you are.

On behalf of the Village,

Cheerio,

Yours,

F.C. Barrett.

POSTSCRIPT

Mr Barrett has very kindly sent me copies of the last three months' News Letters, and I have most thoroughly enjoyed reading them. I hope he will keep my name on his regular list! I am sure that he and Mr Bradfield deserve the heartiest of congratulations on such an enterprising venture. When he sent them Mr Barrett asked me if I would write a Postscript for the October issue; he didn't say what subject I should write about, and I can't think of anything exciting or particularly interesting. I think we'll call it 'A dip into the Past'; for when I read over again the names of so many Girton 'boys', it makes my mind go back to the years 1930–37. I saw again young Harry and Tony Cranfield two little boys waiting in the Church Porch to ask if they might come back into the Choir, from which they had apparently drifted away owing to some rather over-exuberant youthful spirits! Ronnie Lipscombe and Leonard Hales came back as we first knew them in the Sunday School at the age of 7 or 8 years! Then Claude Kidman in India – I can see him so plainly running home from school down the street. Roy Nightingale, Carlos Griffiths, Douglas Piggott – yes and little John McDougal, who *would* make rabbits with his handkerchief when he should have been deep in prayer! And then here again here's George Betson, up and down Church Lane many times a day, with his older more mature brother Horace – yes – and cricket memories of their Uncle Dick. How slow he thought my one and only 50 were in that Final on Magdalene Ground – and it jolly well was too, much as I was enjoying my brief triumph. I can see him now looking out from beneath the scorer's hut and I can also hear him saying – 'well, I won't say what'. Never mind, Dick I always admired you because you were keen – it's keenness and enthusiasm which pulls us through most things. Roy Naylor, sometimes feeling faint and going out of church half-way through – maybe thoughts of the sermon coming? By the way Ronnie Lipscombe, if you are still in Colombo look out for SQ/MS. E.T. Clarke, who runs a N.A.A.F.I. there – his wife has been staying with us for over two years, with nine other London Evacuees – (we shall miss them when the war is over). Here's Roy Ellis, an

The Revd P.N.H. Palmer, former Rector, and his wife

ever present, now a soldier – how we enjoyed those Choir outings to Upware – five miles from anywhere, and now you are many miles 'Upware' somewhere else, but soon maybe you'll all be coming home, but how these names touch a spot and make us feel the march of Time.

Ever since the War started, I have always looked out in case any of you might get posted this way, and one day we were delighted when Harry Cranfield came in to supper. He was stationed a few miles away but unfortunately only for a short while. Sid Gawthrop in a similar way came and looked us up – congratulations on being a Father! And another day Eric Barker marched through the town and happened to spot me in the Market Place, but I was so blind I didn't see him as they went by.

I go into our Canteen here and have ten minutes Family Prayers every Sunday evening, and one night a party of Military Police were in and when I asked them whereabouts they had lately been their answer was 'near Cambridge, in the Girton Men's Institute'!!!

BCE 34 is still going strong on her reduced rations – I'm afraid not on any cricket trips! It wouldn't be fair to you 'out there'. Did you ever hear of one of those funny little coincidences that do sometimes come and make you stare hard? While I still had the L on, and with that expert tutor, Charlie Nightingale (I'm afraid I've purposely left the Mr out – he won't mind!) sitting beside me, we went for one of our first long rides to Norwich, and as we entered the City, an errand boy stopped us, and said 'Can you tell me where Girton Road is?' and sure enough there was a Girton Road in Norwich! And so in our hearts and minds, we find that Girton Road, and to all of us it brings many a happy memory as we dip into the past. I believe I could go on and on, and fill many more pages, for Girton was very kind to us, and many other names come back to us besides those that have been mentioned in these letters. To all of you, the very best of good wishes, and God bless and be with you wherever you may be – and please excuse this scrappy sort of letter, I'm afraid I have enjoyed writing it much more than you will enjoy reading it. It's just eleven o'clock.

Goodnight all. Happy dreams of Girton.

P.N.H. Palmer, September 30th, 1943

6 Church Lane,
Girton.
December 1943

Dear

It is Xmas time once more – the fifth since this most terrible of all wars began – in addition to Xmas time it is a time when most folk review and reflect. Each one of us has his or her own particular thoughts, but we all, I'm sure, agree that Xmas time and war time are incompatible, whether we view it from the Christian standpoint, of brotherly love and Peace on earth, goodwill towards men or from the family circle, when in peace time we are united, and when all the kindly impulses of goodwill are renewed and strengthened. In war these things are obscured, homes are broken, families are separated, men and women are on active service and their children are evacuated

This Xmas however, there is ground for quiet confidence that these grim dark days will soon be behind us, and that before another Xmas dawns we may all have returned once again to peace, and you to your own fireside.

Ron Lipscombe, R.N.

Little has happened in the village since last month, and very few letters have been received by the N.L. We were very much interested to hear that Sid Gawthrop on his return to North Africa met Will Evans, Henry Cornell and Les Impey. Sid was in the same camp as Will, but did not know until the day he had to move on. Will has been in hospital and is still, unfortunately, under the M.O. He wishes to send greetings to all his friends in the forces and those 'down the village'.

In a note Ron Lipscombe mentions that he walked into a club in Ceylon, looked in the Visitors' Book and there was the signature of Tom Cox, Thornton Road, Girton. He made immediate enquiries, but it transpired that Tom had just left. We hope they have since met, as there is so much to talk about when Girton is so far away.

The following note has been supplied to me by Mr C.E. Lintott, it expresses, I think, the feelings of the village to you 'out there'.

The Local Home Guard after their parade on Wednesday, November 10th, suggested that as a mark of appreciation towards the overseas unit recently installed in the Grange some sort of entertainment be provided. The suggestion was quickly taken up and money flowed in from all quarters and it was decided that they be invited to what in 'Civvy Street' would be called a smoking concert. As they were likely to go on leave at any time, arrangements had to be made for the event to take place on Friday November 12th – entailing some hard work for those handling the arrangements – but at 8.15 p.m. there were no less than 90 men of the two units seated, everything having worked out to schedule. The wives of the H.G. rose to the occasion by providing a more than ample supply of sandwiches, rolls and cakes, whilst the H.G. kept the visitors' glasses filled with good ale. Entertainment was provided by G. Grimwood, the Histon magician and ventriloquist, whose magic and cross talk brought roars of laughter from the visitors. L.A.C. Abbott of the R.A.F. gave a marvellous display at speedy caricature in charcoal, whilst telling the usual amusing stories. Sgt. Coe of ours, gave a rendering of two old time military songs. The visitors also decided to take a hand in the entertaining and gave us a musical medley of songs, old and new, including the new war song, which we hope will soon be popular among us all – Lili Malone [sic] – and Kipling's monologues were, as always, given a rousing reception.

Midnight struck, to the surprise of everyone, bringing to a close in the words of the visitors, 'one of the most enjoyable evenings we've had for years'.

Sunday, the 14th November, being the day chosen as Remembrance Day, the soldier visitors joined the Home Guard for Church parade at the Parish Church, the C.O. laying a wreath on the memorial. Mr Dupont, home on leave from the R.A.F., gave the address.

It has been the practice of the N.L. each month, to ask a member of the Village to write a postscript. As it is Xmas time we invited all who have contributed to send greetings to you.

First of these is Mr Bradfield. I should like to say how I enjoyed his co-operation, in the early days, and am delighted to tell you he in his own words is slowly 'running in' his engine.

Mr Bradfield's Greetings:–

Xmas 1943 is well on the way and many of our hopes are still unfulfilled. To wish you a happy time seems rather easy perhaps from one who will probably enjoy the company of his own family and fireside, but I think I can understand something of your thoughts and feelings as you reflect on your circle incomplete. The thoughts of many in the old village will be with you, and we do not forget your part in this grim struggle, on the outcome of which depends all our bright tomorrows. This note gives me the opportunity to thank you for the letters, messages and enquiries that have reached me during the last two months. I am well on the way to recovery.

May the Quartermaster do his best to make your Xmas happy, and may the future hold for you many a happier one in store.

The Chairman of the Parish Council sends greetings:–
May Victory soon bring you safely home to Girton. We here know that what you want when you get home is Beveridge and a Council House. We in Girton will leave nothing undone to see that you get this.
Michael Pease, November 21st, 1943

Mr Garner sends greetings, first as Chairman of the Entertainment Committee, and secondly as Schoolmaster and friend of all:–
Cordial Xmas greetings to all our people serving in H.M. Forces all over the world. Letters received in a continuous stream indicates the pleasure our efforts on their behalf give, and I can assure everyone that the pleasure the Entertainment Committee gets out of the work they do is equally appreciated. Each succeeding meeting brings forward fresh helpers to our cause and I feel that the work being done is doing something slowly but surely towards bringing the people of Girton more together than they have ever been. The whole Committee join in wishing you all 'God speed' and a quick return to your home surroundings.
And now as Headmaster:–
I am also privileged to send you similar greetings from the school. One of my most interesting experiences during the past four years has been to be at the 'sending end' of this kind of work, whereas exactly 25 years ago I was at the 'receiving' end in the wilds of Persia (Iran), and was involved nightly in arguments with my companions as to who should be 'demobbed' first. I have received letters and messages from old pupils who

have covered the same ground and I find their accounts most interesting. I certainly look forward to comparing notes in the near future with these people. The bright spot of my summer holidays was a day early in August when at work in my greenhouse to suddenly turn round and see a soldier in tropical kit, and I am afraid it took me several seconds to recognise Sid Gawthrop. You have doubtless heard what a sensation his arrival caused in the village. The School itself goes on in just about the same old way, but one cannot help being struck with the happy, contented look of well being in each child. Certainly no one would think judging by the look of the scholars that we had already undergone four years of war, and we in Girton have certainly been well favoured by the fortunes of war in that respect. Now I could go on but I am afraid our 'Editor' will complain about the length of this rather disjointed contribution to the N.L. so will close my remarks with all good wishes to you all wherever you may be, and a quick safe return.

My scholars also join in good wishes and have taken their own way of sending them.

The six years olds (Girls):–

I am a little girl of six yeres old. I hope you have a very merry Cristmas and a happy new yere. I hope you all will soon be with us again and the war will be over quickle. This is all from the six yeres old.

Girton Schoolchildren old and young, at the 1946 Centenary

The six years olds (Boys):–
Dear Soldiers, Salors, and Airmen, I am a little boy of six years old. I hope the war will soon be over so you will come back. I wish you all a merry Cristmas and a happy new year. Best wishes to you all from all the six and seven years old at Girton school.

The eight year olds:–
We the 'eight year olds' of Girton School, and we are writing to you all, soldiers, sailors and airmen of Girton to wish you a very happy Christmas. We feel sorry for those of you who have to fight for us or go out on dark cold nights in aeroplanes, and we hope you are well and safe. Hurry up and finish the war and come home again.
With very best wishes, from
The 'eight year olds'

The ten year olds:–
We wish you all, in the army and the navy and the airforce all over the world a happy Christmas. We expect you find a lot of interesting things in other countries. We have socials, dances and concerts to raise money so we can send you little gifts, and hope you will soon be back in Girton with all your friends and relations to enjoy them with us. We read in the papers and hear on the news what wonderful things you soldiers, sailors and airmen are doing. We all hope this letter will cheer you up a bit.
The Ten Year Olds

The Revd L.G. Tucker, Rector

Mrs Leakey sends greetings:–
Mr Barrett has of late allowed me to give some small help with the News Letter. I think many others beside myself feel more closely knit in the friendship of the village than ever before, the village never thinks of itself without including you. So Christmas greetings to you all.
H. Wilfrida Leakey

The Rector sends greetings:–
May your Christmas be all the happier, since you have such good

hope of home again before another Christmas. It is through your prowess that the hope is so strong. God bless you and your families here. I think I may say we are all full of hope and that makes us as happy as we can be till you come back.
Your sincere friend,
L.G. Tucker.

Miss Wallis sends greetings:–
To wish all the members of His Majesties Forces from Girton – both men and women wherever they may be – the very best of good wishes for Xmas and the New Year, with the hope that you will all soon be home with us again.

Mr Sterndale Burrows – you will remember his postscript 'The Church Clock' – sent me what he called a Vignette for inclusion in this letter. I sincerely regret that space does not allow its inclusion. However, here is his accompanying note.
I would convey my best wishes to our serving men for Xmas and the New Year. A few words to encourage them, to lift up their hearts and keep their faces towards the dawn. They need our help in whatsoever way we can give it – above all to save them from despondency. May God bless them all, and the messages you are sending them.
Yours sincerely
Sterndale Burrows

Finally may I be allowed to add my greetings. I have had grand fun writing these letters, I only hope they have been of interest and if you wish them to continue I am more than repaid for my trouble.
May I convey my best wishes to you for Xmas and the New Year – may you soon be back amongst us as we miss you and need you, and long for the day of your return.
On behalf of the Village,
Yours,
F.C. Barrett.

6 Church Lane,
Girton.
January 1944

Dear

First, on behalf of the village, may I wish you a happy New Year; to many of you in difficult situations the word 'happy' may seem at first somewhat out of place at the present moment, but is it really? We at home are full of hope that this year will see the conclusion of the war in Europe, if so, it will mean that some of you will be returning home to your loved ones, those made dear and more precious by the parting, and also to the communal life of the old village. Naturally the homecoming will cause great rejoicing and there will be many personal things to attend to such as the adjustment of your lives to civilian employment and getting the house and garden back into working order. But what then, what of the future? What sort of life shall we expect, what sort of education shall we desire for our children, what sort of house do we want and how shall we spend our leisure time? All these things are dependent upon what Beveridge calls 'A minimum standard of living', therefore it is imperative that this cardinal point must be established as soon after hostilities as possible. One of the main objects of the N.L. has been to place these points before you for your consideration so that when you come home you will have crystallised your requirements, and together we can go forward. As you know already, things generally have stood still, there have been no more houses, the sewage scheme has had to be postponed, and our school building is 100 years old and requires modernising; the proposed alteration and enlargement of the Village Institute has also been postponed, and so we could go on giving examples of things which have stood still. The one great point however is that the war has taught our village people the art of co-operating one with another, their unity and comradeship are, I'm sure, equal to that which you are experiencing on the field of battle. This then is a sure foundation on which to build our bright tomorrows, and I think we can go forward together with hope and sober confidence that the future will not be half so dark as some will have us believe, but at the same time it will not be so rosy either, rather we shall reap from the future according to the amount of thought and good will which each one of us is now willing to contribute. The N.L. has in the past asked readers at home and abroad to send in their thoughts and ideas so that we may discuss them together. So far we have not yet received any letters relating to this subject, we realise that you have little time or comfort to sit down and put your thoughts on paper, but if you can possibly find the time to do so we would appreciate them.

Last month as I was delivering the N.L. I was struck by the number of women readers on my list. We are inclined to forget the part they are playing, and I felt that you would like to hear something about them. As far as I can gather there are 12 serving with H.M. Forces and the W.L.A. We send our congratulations to Miss Elspeth Macalister who has obtained a commission in the W.A.A.F. and to her sister Jean who has also obtained a commission in the A.T.S. Jean is an interpreter, stationed in Cairo, recently she has been ill with Yellow Jaundice, we hope that by now she has fully recovered. Misses D. Green, P. Hunt and M. Rudd are in the W.A.A.F., Miss C. Engledow is in the W.R.N.S., Miss K. Parfitt in the A.T.S., Miss M. Rudd in the F.A.N.Y.S., the Misses M. Engledow, J. Watson and Mrs Harrington (nee King) are in the W.L.A. and finally Miss Mitham is serving with N.A.A.F.I. You will see we have a representative from the village in each branch of the women's services. And speaking of the part our women are playing we must not forget your wives, they are often left alone or with small children. It never struck me how lonely they must be until recently whilst I was delivering the N.L. to your homes during the dark winter evenings. I often knock at a door, in reply a voice from within calls 'Who's there'? and until a reassuring word has been given they don't unbolt the door. You should be proud of them for they carry on with dignity and in silence.

Mary Rudd, W.A.A.F.

On the 8th December the Youth Centre Advisory Committee met in order to review and reflect upon the past terms work of the Youth Centre and also to plan future arrangements. The Youth Centre is part of the Service of Youth administered by the Education Committee, it is a new service which has been organised since the outbreak of war, and its purpose is to interest and further educate the 14–21 year-olds in citizenship. I have had the honour to organise and be the leader of the Girton Centre since its inception three years ago. I have been assisted by a group of loyal helpers, chief amongst them Mrs H.W. Leakey. It has been most interesting to watch the development of our adolescents who begin to show a real sense of communal responsibility. They have a drama and discussion group, popular lectures are arranged, as well as monthly educational films. The centre meets on two evenings of the week and has in addition to the above activities, a canteen and the usual recreational facilities. Previous to the meeting of the Adult Committee on December 8th our local centre had worked in its own way and alone, now, however, we have established a liaison with Impington Village College by electing Mr Parr, the warden, and Mr Tyack, the new adult organiser at the College, on to our committee. Hitherto Cambridgeshire's Education Committee's experiment based on the Village College idea has been watched with great interest by the rest of the country. Usually a Village College is established in the centre of approximately ten villages, these contribute all their children between 11 years of age and

Cadets on parade at Impington Village College

school-leaving age to the College where they should get a higher and more specialised education than could be given them with the facilities obtainable in their own village. The College also provided all the adult education for the contributory villages, these adults being transported to the College by means of buses which made a circular tour of the villages on several evenings of the week. Since the war transport has been reduced to one bus a week, and the villages have had to organise their own activities. Mr Parr and his colleague Mr Tyack informed our committee that the future policy of the college would be for their instructors and lecturers to come out to the village as well as the villagers going to the college. In future the more specialised activities such as Language Teaching, a festival of drama and music, or crafts where special tools are required would be held at the College. Girton has been chosen as the first village for this change of policy and Mr Tyack, who has been doing similar work in the Linton area, will give the first lecture in the Village Institute on January 19th.

Before leaving this subject I should like you to know the names of our excellent advisory committee – the Chairman, Mrs Leakey, is supported by Miss Hibbert-Ware, Miss Murray, assistant Tutor of Girton College, Miss Ellis a Welfare and Housing Officer of the Cambridge Borough and Mrs Goddard, who as a comparative new comer to the village has given invaluable help. On the men's side we have Mr Garner who you all know, Dr Eric Smith, University lecturer in Invertebrate Zoology, Mr Booth, Headmaster of Littleton House School, Mr Bradfield, Mr Parr and Mr Tyack representatives of Impington Village College, with myself as secretary.

You will recall in last month's N.L. we gave you an account of how the Village Home Guard entertained troops from overseas. When the party was over it was found that the H.G. were slightly out of pocket, they let this fact be quietly known amongst their friends, the immediate result was that the deficit was settled and a nice balance in hand. The next question was what to do with the balance. A small committee was formed from the platoon and it was decided to give a party to all the children of school age in the village. On Wednesday 22nd December the H.G. Headquarters resounded with shouts of delight as the children first enjoyed an excellent tea which was followed by real ice cream, films and games, community singing completed a first rate evening. Congratulations, Home Guard, if you haven't had a chance at the enemy you certainly have brought pleasure to our children.

Girton is not a wealthy village, but I think it is certainly above the average for giving a helping hand to a deserving cause, this has been demonstrated during the past week by the amount of money raised. 'Jim' Ison, that indefatigable worker on behalf of others, organised, with the aid of Mr Walter Garner, a mock auction in the 'Old Crown', the money raised was given to the prisoners of war fund. Mr Butler of Histon auctioned the goods and during the course of the evening extracted £23.11.6d. in a most lighthearted manner from the willing purchasers.

The Women's Institute also held a sale of goods which were made by their make-do-and-mend meetings in order to raise funds for their Federation. Their efforts were crowned with success and they were able to send £10.0.0 to their Federation and also to give the Village Entertainment Committee £5 to be used for and on behalf of those serving with H.M. Forces.

A Whist drive was organised by the Youth Centre in order to present their members serving with the Forces with a small Xmas box as a token of remembrance and affection. A profit of £8.8.0d was made, so our nine members have by now received, we hope, a postal order for 17/6d.

A concert was also held in the village, Alice Reynold's 'Highlights of Variety' presented an enjoyable programme which was thoroughly enjoyed by a packed Institute, including our troops from overseas who were the guests of the Entertainment Committee. In addition to all the artists giving their services, Messrs J. and H. Ison of Histon Road, gave a magnificent cockerel for a Xmas draw, this brought in the handsome sum of £3.10.0.

Our local N.F.S. men also held a Whist drive in aid of their benevolent fund, this too was a great success, so you can see from these few examples how my earlier remarks about the villagers' unity and comradeship is borne out in a practical way.

Many of you will be pleased to hear that that well known character, Mr Charles Nightingale, is convalescing in the Village after a serious operation. I'm sure you all wish him a speedy recovery to health and strength.

The news from India that an old stalwart with the cricket bat Jack Balaam has met Cyril 'Son' Wilson has brought much pleasure here at home. These two most likeable lads would have plenty of notes to compare for it is over two years since they left these shores, and probably three or four since they saw each other. Before Jack went abroad he was stationed in Yorkshire, and by all accounts he distinguished himself with the 'willow' in that county of cricketers. News has also been received from Les Impey, who is in Italy, Stan (Diddley) Hankin who is with B.N.A.F., both send their kind regards and best wishes to all their friends at home and abroad. Letters and cards have also been received from Miss M. Engledow, Roy 'Midge' Ellis, Cliff Hankin and Robt Burrows.

Jack Balaam

It was grand to meet Tony Cranfield home on leave after his exciting time of assisting with the Salerno landings. I enjoyed hearing his hopes and fears about future prospects after the war, he certainly must have given it considerable thought for he mentioned it at his cousin's Miss Jean Watson's 21st birthday party where we were thoroughly enjoying ourselves.

The only other person who was home on leave for Xmas was our old friend Roy 'Gummy' Naylor, looking very fit and well.

That is all the news for this month, don't forget to write if you possibly can find the time to do so. Finally I should like to send you best wishes and lots of luck for 1944.

Yours,
F.C. Barrett.

6 Church Lane,
Girton.
February 1944

Dear

In the Village speculation and hopes rise higher as each day passes. Everyone seems to think that when the second front opens the war will soon be won. That may or may not be, but never-the-less people are hoping to see you all returning home sometime this year with victory in your pocket from the European war. Since you all have helped the second time in a quarter of a century to turn defeat into victory, you also, that is if you so desire, must have a say in the peace. You will remember that after the last war there was an immediate boom, and an appearance of prosperity, but in a short time the most real of all War Memorials was a monstrous army of workless men. This fact is obviously uppermost in the minds of you all, for during the past week one of our national papers has published a survey on what you wanted most after the war. Approximately 51% wanted a job, 23% wanted a decent house to live in and only 3% were willing to put Education and Beveridge first. Some of you will feel that Girton is not an industrial area and as most folk will be readily absorbed into general employment it will be no concern of ours what goes on in other towns. Without attempting to preach a sermon it is the concern of all of us what happens to other people in other towns and for that matter in other countries. Sentimental meditations upon the glories of a problematic Utopia will not help us to solve these difficulties. We no longer live in a world the future of which we can leave to itself, that policy went out when steam and electricity came in, and when it became possible to speak to our neighbours at the other side of the world in a couple of minutes. Thus far we have always lived as if we were an accident – but when you come to think of it, is there any difference between the world at large and our own town or village? If there is any difference it is one of quantity rather than quality, and that is all! The opportunity for Girton to get down to this question of world citizenship, to know something about other countries and to tolerate ideas foreign to us will be given on Wednesday next when Mr P.C.N. Tyack, M.A., the new adult organiser to Impington Village College, delivers a lecture in the Village Institute entitled 'America, Russia and the Future'. Should there be sufficient interest, further weekly lectures will be arranged and a discussion group formed to study such problems in greater detail.

A month or two ago an Allotments and Gardening Association was formed in the village, a very representative committee was elected with Mr J.H. Garner as Chairman, Mr S.A. Lawrence, Secretary, and Mr C.E. Lintott as Treasurer. The objects of the Association are to promote the interests of allotment holders and gardeners, to co-operate with local authorities and other bodies having as their objective the provision of lime, basic slag, seeds, potatoes, fertilisers, tools, etc. for members. In addition to this the association undertakes to arrange lectures, discussions and general instruction in horticulture. Already the members have had the opportunity of seeing a film on horticulture, hearing a lecture on soil fertility, and we understand that in the near future a demonstration on how to prune fruit trees will be given by Mr Cramp, the County Horticulture adviser, in the orchard at Littleton House School.

On January 4th the Entertainment Committee gave a party to all children of school age in the village. It really was a treat to see such a collection of healthy and well cared for children. We are sure that there may be equal, but not finer, children in the land. After tea the children amused each other by coming on to the stage reciting poetry, singing songs or dancing a jig. Here again one felt proud of them and their ability, no one need fear for our rising generation. The party was brought to a close with an amusing film of Mickey Mouse and one of Laurel and Hardy, these brought shrieks of laughter, such as only happy children can produce. As each child left to go home they were presented with two sixpenny savings stamps to add to their collection.

The boys of Littleton House School produced and presented their own concert to a private audience on January 8th. Being a nigger concert it was appropriately called the Black-Out-Minstrels. Negro songs were sung and the boys gave a P.T. display which demonstrated their skill and the careful preparation of the masters. The village people will have an opportunity to see this show on Thursday the 20th, a shilling will be charged for admission and the proceeds are to be given to local P.O.W. Littleton House school has kindly invited all the village children to come to the show and a film on Saturday afternoon free of charge.

The friends of Walter Dixon, who is a prisoner of war in Japanese hands, will be pleased to hear that a postcard was received from him on Xmas eve. It stated that he was well and that people at home should not worry about him. The postcard was dated sometime in February 1942 – that gives you some idea of postal difficulties.

Some of you will already have read with pleasure that Professor Engledow, Professor of Agriculture in the University and a resident of the village, has been honoured by the King with a knighthood for his services to Agriculture. The professor takes an active interest in the life of the village, being a school manager, a member of the church council and a major in the Home Guard.

During the past month our clerk to the Parish Council, Mr Tom Palmer has been called up for duties with the R.A.F. In his absence Mr C.E. Lintott will act as clerk, and also as salvage officer.

Many of you will be interested to hear that the time has come for Tom and Dick, the two inseparable twins to render further service to their country. It seems as though it was but yesterday that these mischievous identical twins were attending the village school. Dick is entering the Navy, but Tom has to go with his pal Roland Wilson to the coal mines. We all realise that coal is important and the supply position is acute, but it does seem unfortunate that these two lads who were such enthusiastic members of the Cadet Force, they attended parades on two evenings a week and gave up their only week's annual leave in order to attend camp, are now directed, without question to the mines. Many people are asking why the scheme which has been provided for the girls, namely if they have served 6 months in the G.T.C. they are given preference for the Forces, should not also be applied to the boys of the pre-service training units. Speaking personally I have always disagreed with the policy of the Cadet Force, it seems wrong to me to make a boy of $13\frac{1}{2}$ years of age into a miniature soldier, if on the other hand these boys were given plenty of games and P.T. to make them fit and agile they would now have been prepared to adapt themselves equally to mines or the forces. Nevertheless I am convinced that the sending of boys from all classes and from all parts of the country to the mines, will not only do them good, but will render the miners a great service by getting them improved conditions of work, so that our lads will be proud of the day they left home.

During the past month the N.L. has received a welcome airgraph from Carlos Griffiths, he is at an advanced base in the Indian Command. He tells us that he enjoys the N.L. and looks forward to hearing how his pals are getting on. He says 'The Jungle is most interesting, snakes abound, beautiful butterflies flit about and the trees and flowers are quite different from those which one is used to seeing at home'. Another long letter comes from Tom Pauley, serving with M.E.F. Tom tells me that he has recovered from his wound. When he wrote his letter he was passing through Palestine and he says 'I wonder what the children of Girton would do if they were suddenly placed in these orange groves?'. Tom continues to make my mouth water with descriptions of grape vines on the Arabs' houses. Still, in spite of this, he says 'I'd give anything to stand again on the road and look at that old clock which Mr Burrows spoke about'.

Finally Lt. Jack Wakelin writes from the North of England to say that the N.L. is passed round the officer's mess each month, and that the officers are getting interested in Girton. Jack was one of the first to join up from the village, he was quickly promoted to Staff Quarter-master Sergeant, after seeing service in Iceland he returned to England, and then was commissioned.

Mr J.H. Garner, as chairman of the Entertainment Committee has received quite a number of letters thanking the Committee for the Xmas present sent to them by the Village. We had hoped to tell you where each one was stationed and how they were, but I'm afraid space will not allow it. Nevertheless we think Ken Mayes in the North of England summed up the thoughts of you all when he said 'Perhaps next Xmas will be a happier one, in any case we shall be content to carry on until it is finished, with the knowledge that we have loyal friends at home to support us.'

Sgt Ken Mayes

The postscript this month is written by an old friend, Sidney Chaplin. Sidney is a drainage officer for the Cambridgeshire War Agriculture Committee, many of you will remember him as ambulance driver for the Girton First-Aid party. Since the party was disbanded he joined a Home Guard Ack Ack battery, and has since been promoted Sergeant, and only the other day he received the congratulations of the officer commanding the area for passing his tests with distinction, and has also I believe been recommended for a commission.

That is all for this month, lots of luck and best wishes.
Yours sincerely,
F.C. Barrett.

POSTSCRIPT

On starting to write this I realise more than ever how different this village of ours is from most in that it is divided into two sections – the old village mostly agricultural and the new with its main interest in Cambridge, but there is one interest common to both and that is food. And so my excuse for risking boring those of you who are not interested in agriculture is that you are at least interested in food! Most of you will know that home production of arable crops has increased very considerably during the war.

A Steam Threshing Machine, part of the 'new' agriculture

This has been brought about at the expense of much good grassland, of course, but also there are hundreds of acres of derelict land, bush or swamp which have been brought under the plough with the aid of the Excavators, Bulldozers and Gyrotillers now quite common sights in the county, and many of you when you return after a long absence will on looking over the garden hedge see a very different view from what you were used to seeing before the war, though that does not apply so much to

Girton as to many other Cambridgeshire villages. This is because Girton, even in the worst of the farming depression, owing to its position near Cambridge, the nature of its subsoil and its reasonable land drainage (not to be confused with its house drainage!) never was allowed to go back to its semi-natural state of bush and scrub. It was the real heavy clay lands of Croydon wilds, Hatley wilds and Graveley roughs which really went back to nature and were in places so densely bushed as to make them impenetrable at many places. Most of these areas are now growing their second and third crops and are showing what heavy land will do when it is drained and well cultivated.

Other large areas which have been brought into cultivation are in the Cambridgeshire Fens. Here, of course, the problems were very different from those of the heavy lands, and the chief difficulties to be overcome were water and bog oaks. These areas had in almost all cases been drained before, but the windmills used for pumping the water out had become useless with age, and the areas became completely waterlogged again. Diesel engines now do the work of the windmills and many miles of dykes have been re-opened to bring the water to the pumps. As the fens become drained the level of the land falls, and the great oak trees which have lain for hundreds of years well below the surface become dangerous to implements and have to be dug or blown out of the ground. These great relics of our old forests are as sound and harder than when they first fell, probably when the soldiers of that day were putting on their woad to resist the first invasion of this island! and but for the power of modern equipment they might well prove insurmountable obstacles.

To-day this land, clay and fen, is growing record crops, but what of the future? Will they again be allowed to fall back to bush and swamp and to be an eyesore to the countryman and a disgrace to the country? Two things, it seems to me, will decide this – profitable agriculture and a return of our people to the land. The second of these is dependent on the first, for few can afford the luxury of farming without profit and the farm-worker cannot receive the adequate wage so long denied him in the past unless the prices received for the result of his labours are also adequate. These problems are being faced; let us hope that this time a solution will be found which will ensure a prosperous future for our oldest and largest industry.

S.H.C.

6 Church Lane,
Girton.
March 1944

Dear

March is here again and with its advent we celebrate our first anniversary. A year ago the N.L. was born, the first copy was printed and distributed to a few village men serving with H.M. Forces. Many of you who did not receive that copy may be interested to know how the N.L. came into being, the purpose behind its publication and how it has developed in this past year.

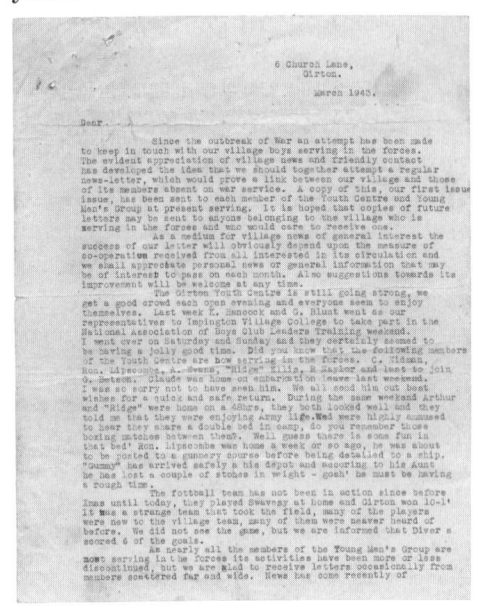

The first Newsletter, March 1943

During the winter of the second year of war the Girton Youth Centre was inaugurated, it soon began to grow and feel its feet and we had many happy evenings together, but like every other organisation we were touched by the heavy hand of war. As the boys became 18 years of age they were called up, and their going was always an occasion for a farewell party and after the general fond farewells we promised them that we'd write and keep them in touch with the village and with each other.

After a while, as more of our lads joined the forces, we found it an exacting task to keep in touch with them all. We realised the interest too of news and of the general gossip of the village, especially to the men overseas, and we were determined to maintain our contact. It was decided that the best solution to this problem was to write a general letter each month and have it duplicated, and despatched to all concerned. One Sunday afternoon Mr H. Bradfield called upon me and in general conversation I placed before him our scheme, he asked if he too could be allowed to co-operate so that he might also be able to send a copy to each member of the Young Man's Group; this was agreed and during the following month the first short letter was composed.

On looking up the first letter, I believe a couple of dozen copies were distributed — you may be interested to know that our circulation has risen to 80–90 copies each month — what we said then still holds good. We stated that 'The evident appreciation of village news and friendly contact has developed the idea that we should attempt a regular news-letter which would prove a link between our village and those of its members absent on war service. As a medium for village news of general interest the success of our letter will obviously depend upon the measure of co-operation received in its circulation and we shall appreciate personal news or general information that may be of interest to pass on each month. Also suggestions towards its improvement will be welcome at any time.'

It is grand to look back over the past year and recall with pleasure the generous help we have received from friends at home and in the forces, especially those abroad and far away.

To you all on this our first birthday we send our cordial greetings, very many thanks for those letters and good wishes. We wish you all good luck and a quick and safe return.

It is with deep regret and sorrow that we have to record the death of Miss Hibbert-Ware. We were all shocked to hear that she had had a stroke and as her life lay in the balance, small groups of people could be seen about the village discussing her condition, or asking, almost in whispers, how she was. After a week of suspense the end came. It seemed impossible; it couldn't be true; the villagers and all the birds and beasts, things she loved seemed hushed and quiet. Truly, as a correspondent to our local paper put it 'Mourning in the village dwells'.

At the end of this letter you will find an appreciation of Miss Hibbert-Ware, it has been written by Mrs H.W. Leakey and we are sure it expresses our feelings.

During the past month we have had productions of music and drama which raise hopes for the future. First, the village ladies choral group gave, with the aid of very gifted friends from Cambridge, an excellent concert in the Village Institute on Sunday 30th January. Those who had the pleasure of attending this particular concert were agreed that it was one of the most enjoyable yet presented on a Sunday evening. Mr L.N. Tingey and his choir can congratulate themselves on the admirable and varied programme, and they can be assured that they will be well supported in any similar venture.

On February 4th the Youth Centre presented what they termed an Evening's Entertainment which also included Tolstoi's one act play called 'Michael', a fine play and an ambitious undertaking. Out of a total of 25, no less than 16 members of the Centre took part in the production. The programme was divided into two parts, the first half was of a lively boisterous nature, it included community singing, dramatic sketches by the boys, duets by Misses Maureen Cranfield and Dorothy Fergerson, and an accordion medley by Neville King who is also chairman of the Centre. The second half consisted of a pianoforte solo played by a very good friend of the Centre, Mrs Goddard, and the play which was presented by the Drama Group under the supervision of Miss E. Ellis. The theme of the play shows that Michael an outcast from heaven is sent to earth to learn three truths – what dwells in man, what is not given to man and what man lives by. The part of Matryona was played with feeling and understanding by Miss Betty Farrow, her husband Simon by Tony Blunt and their daughter Anuska by Pamela Cornell. Michael was portrayed by Mrs P. Love, whilst that of the arrogant nobleman and his servant by Ken Hancock and Russell Jaggard respectively. Miss Grace Evans was the woman who adopted two children – Ann and Janet White. The realistic and colourful costumes added to a well produced and enjoyable play and great credit is due to all concerned. At the invitation of Miss E. Round, the County Youth Organiser, the whole performance was reproduced at Impington Village College the next evening in order to demonstrate the possibilities of drama in a rural Youth Centre to the Boy Leader's Training Conference. The profits from both these productions have been devoted to the fund in aid of our villagers serving with H.M. Forces.

In a recent N.L. whilst mentioning the names of our serving women we regret that by an oversight, we failed to mention that Mrs Peirce (nee E. Pauley) is and has been a member of the N.F.S. almost since the outbreak of war. Mrs Stan Dixon (nee J. Bonsor) was also a member of the W.L.A. but has had to resign thro' ill health. She recently underwent a serious operation, but we are glad to say that she has almost recovered.

The N.L. has pleasure in congratulating her husband who has recently been promoted to Ft/Lt., and also Roy Nightingale, who is in the R.A.F., on his promotion to the rank of corporal.

Letters and airgraphs have been received from far and near during the past month. In a long letter from H.L. Rooke, somewhere in Iraq, he says 'I can hardly say how much I enjoy reading the N.L. and eagerly await the arrival of the next copy'. He is delighted to hear of the whereabouts of members of his Scout Group, many of you will recall that he shared with Mr Rule the honour of being the Scout Leader of the village. He continues 'I desire to send them all my very best wishes and tell them that after the war, and after our ultimate return I am going to organise a magnificent Scouts reunion in the village and I am looking forward to seeing you all there'.

A letter from Frank Dupont, who is for the moment stationed nearer home, says 'You cannot fully realise what the N.L. means when one is far away. I remember one letter arriving while I was at home on leave, and I read it through with much interest. Going back to my Island Station the next week I took it with me and then read it again. The interest and enjoyment caused in those far surroundings was much greater than that of the first reading I can assure you'. I should like to express through the N.L. my very best wishes to all the boys, wherever they are. An airgraph from Ronny Lipscombe, who is still in Ceylon, also sends greetings and best wishes.

Harry Chapman sends greetings to all his pals. Harry has been in N. Africa and was one of 30 selected from his regiment to form a guard of honour when Mr Churchill reviewed our victorious army in Tunis. He is now in Italy and says the mud has to be seen to be believed, it is far worse than anything we have ever seen at home.

News has been received from Ron Cole in Malta and from Jack Collings who has returned home from America where he has been stationed for the last six months.

Well that will be all for this month, we send you our best wishes and kind regards. Keep smiling and don't be long before you return home.
Lots of luck,
Cheerio.
[There is no signature]

Miss Hibbert-Ware – An Appreciation

The spare swift moving figure of Miss Hibbert-Ware will no longer be seen about our village. In that short sentence lies the grief of almost everyone in Girton.

The children loved her because she opened for them the windows of nature's magic world. Through her they learnt to recognise the stoat from the weasel, to hear the thrush, who sings his song twice over, to know the grass snake as a friend. Trees, flowers, all living things were their bond.

The Parish Council has lost perhaps its wisest member and surest friend. Impington College, the School here and Mr Garner will go to her no longer for the counsel of a fellow teacher, experienced, kindly, possessed of a vision wherein teaching was a sharing of fine experiences, never a dull routine of pedagoging.

The Women's Institute mourns for its friend who never spared herself, who could light in others her ever shining enthusiasm for the loveliest things of mind and spirit. No longer will she help with school dinners, while children chatter to her of all they have seen or found in the countryside. Paper may still be salvaged but she will not be the one to undertake and organise the job that no one else cared to do.

She lived gladly with a fullness of life that few achieve. She died after a week of illness, without suffering. On the last day of her fully conscious life she had completed the first half of a new piece of research on Curlews. Faith she had, but it was in her works that we all learnt to love her.

Miss Alice Hibbert-Ware

Her passing leaves the village so much the poorer, but our grief must turn to keeping alive the things for which she most cared.

Coleridge's lines came to me as I sit and write of her tonight:–
'Farewell, Farewell! but this I tell
To thee, thou Wedding-Guest!
He prayeth well, who loveth well
Both man and bird and beast.
He prayeth best who loveth best
All things both great and small,
For the dear God who loveth us,
He made and loveth all'.

6 Church Lane,
Girton.
April 1944

Dear

Since last I wrote to you I have as usual had my ear cocked ready to receive any item of village news so I may be able to pass it on to you. I am sorry to say that there is little to tell; life has gone on as usual, so much so that I have practically nothing to report. While this dearth of news has persisted I wondered what on earth I could write about, I thought that I could give you an account of the village scene in April, how the hedge rows are bursting into leaf, and how the gardens and allotments are springing into life, but could I honestly do this when I have to write this letter in early March for you to receive it in April? As yet the snowdrops and crocuses are still in bloom, the hedges are only showing but the faintest trace of green, and so far as the allotments are concerned the late gardeners, like myself, have still to finish their winter digging. Others are more fortunate, they have planted broad beans, shallots and onions, and now may be seen examining the ground most carefully to see if the seeds have germinated and are coming through.

It is light now in the evening almost to 7.30 p.m.; as I sit at home having my evening meal, and provided it is not too cold, I have the windows open and look across to the Recreation Ground and listen, but alas! the old familiar figures and sounds are missing. How many of you can recall the days when you hurried home from work, swallowed your tea and rushed up to the Recreation Ground to have a kick at the football before darkness fell? How I used to enjoy those practices, we used to play partners or forwards versus the backs and the goal-keeper, but should sufficient men turn up we'd 'pick up' and play for all we were worth without referee or linesman. Gradually as darkness fell, first one and then another would leave the field, until only a few, who I'm sure must have possessed cat's eyes, continued to flit about like bats, you could only tell their whereabouts by an occasional dull thud of a boot striking the ball, or the happy laughter as the game descended into a combination of soccer and rugger. Now the Rec is quiet; it is impossible to purchase a new football without a permit, and those which occasionally find their way onto the Rec, are almost worn out, furthermore there are very few people available to play football, those who remain are either too old or too busy.

The Village Football Team, including many of the recipients of this letter

Many of you have asked how the village football team is getting on. I am sorry to say that we cannot raise a team, two or three of our village lads play for Histon Institute in the Minor League and have contributed to that team's success in not losing a single match this season.

You may be interested to hear how good resulted from evil intent? During a recent alert an almost brand new enemy plane came floating over the house-tops of an East Anglian town and settled itself in the back gardens of the houses of a recently built estate. It came so quietly and alighted so gently that the occupants of the houses did not hear this pilotless machine land, it was found by a warden who reported it to Central Control, who in turn warned the unsuspecting householders. These good people were naturally surprised to find this machine invading their privacy, but they quickly recovered their composure and were soon shaking Red Cross collecting boxes in front of would be sightseers. Although it was only a matter of days before the machine was dismantled and removed, these enterprising people had collected no less than £100. They have now announced that they have given £20 to the Merchant Seamen's comfort fund, and £80 to the Red Cross Society.

During the past month we have received letters from, and heard about, quite a number of the lads and lassies from our village. First let me tell you about what we have heard, and then deal with the letters later.

Will Evans has arrived in the village from N. Africa looking suntanned and very fit. He came to see me today and told me that he would drink to the health of all the Girton lads in the local tonight and wish them an equally speedy return home.

Tom Impey has arrived in India, he says 'he is well and at the moment has a comfortable billet in addition to good food'. Robt Burrows has turned up in the Azores with the R.A.F., and Ron Cole has apparently left Malta and was last heard of in Algeria. And now for the letters:–

The first one came from Miss Parfitt who is in an Ack Ack Battery somewhere in the Midlands. In a very charming and interesting letter she asks me to thank all in the village who have contributed towards her happiness in the forces, and says 'that when she returns home she will endeavour to return some of the kindness shown to her'. 'Midge' Ellis wrote to thank the Youth Centre for his Xmas present, which came as a pleasant surprise to him. He says 'You seem to be losing your older members, but I do hope that new ones are coming along to keep the club going'. He too sends greetings to all his friends and looks forward to meeting them again in the 'Old Village'. Our only marine, Roy Naylor wrote to say that after a number of moves he is now aboard H.M.S. Nelson. 'Really', he says, 'you wouldn't know it was a ship, it is more like a floating barracks.' Finally 'Gummy' sends greetings to all at home and abroad, and adds that he is fit and full of high spirits – not rum – he is not yet old enough to receive this ration.

A letter and a magazine of the Royal Air Force in British Columbia was received with pleasure from S. Huddlestone who is at Sidney B.C. Canada. In his letter he says, 'I must congratulate you on the job of work you are doing for the boys of the village, I expect they look forward each month to the N.L. as I do. I for one hope you will be able to keep it up, for I think I can surely say that we all appreciate it.' He continues, 'I had my first leave at Vancouver, and I thoroughly enjoyed my stay in that city. It is a very nice place but at present only one place I would like to see and that little place on the map is called Girton'. On looking through the magazine, which is an excellent production, I enjoyed reading it very much, I found that Mr Huddlestone has been presented with a Dominion Marksman's Bronze Medal for Rifle shooting. Congratulations, and best wishes from us all.

The final letter from our serving men came from Q.M.S. E.J. Stearn; before I quote from his long and interesting letter I should like to tell Mr Stearn that I see his sturdy son John every day, and that he and I are becoming great friends, he is a grand lad, and only today I watched him helping his Grandfather dig your garden. You will be surprised and proud of him when you return home, when you went away he was, I believe, in long clothes.

Mr Stearn says 'Much has happened and many miles have been traversed since I wrote to you last year. I think at that time I was seeing Tommy Pauley. Tommy was sent off on a Cook's course, and was returning to my station when I was posted, so I missed him. We corresponded for a while, but then work came in so fast that there was no time for writing and we lost track of each other, but I was delighted the other day when one of his letters caught up with me, it turns out that he is not far away from here, though I doubt if we can arrange a meeting'. Tom tells me he's very well and that he is about to take a more advanced cook's course – 'I tell him he will be useful to his wife when he returns home'.

I should like to quote a great deal more from Mr Stearn's letter, but space does not permit. Amongst many interesting things he says he has been thousands of miles in the desert, to Benghazi, then back to Egypt where he met Basil Wallis from St Margaret's Rd, and although they did not spend much time together, they had a grand chat about Girton. 'Basil' he says 'is well and sends his best wishes, and thoroughly enjoys reading the N.L.'. Mr Stearn continues 'I was favoured on Xmas Eve in that I was able to get to Bethlehem. I wanted to get to a service, but time forbade.' An excellent description Bethlehem, the crypt where Christ was supposed to be born, the countryside round about, and an account of what he had for Xmas dinner follows next, I'd better not quote the menu, all I can say is that it was a superfluous statement when Mr Stearn says 'They enjoyed themselves'. At the end of this long and interesting letter he concludes 'As a souvenier of the war I think the N.L. with the postscripts should be bound and made purchaseable in volume form, and here is order No.1.'

To you all many thanks for your most welcome letters. Do keep writing, as we are most anxious to hear about you, your joys and sorrows, your difficulties and good times, it is all anxiously awaited here – to all of you who have never written – what about a few lines?

Here at home, in Parliament, in Rural and District Councils and Parish Councils, one of the foremost topics is housing after the war. Many of you on reading Mr Pease's Xmas message in which he said 'what you want when you get home is Beveridge and a Council house' replied 'What sort of a council house?'

Miss Ellis, who has written this month's postscript, lives in Girton, and is a Housing and Welfare Officer for the Borough of Cambridge. She has had a very wide experience in this type of work. Miss Ellis is willing to help anyone in our village to find the right way to approach the responsible authorities, so that prospective tenants may be able to help themselres to get the house they desire. After reading her postscript I'm sure you will desire to hear, in more detail, further facts about housing.

With best wishes,
Sincerely yours,
F.C. Barrett.

POSTSCRIPT

Mr Barrett has asked me to write the postscript on Housing. This is far too big a subject to deal with in detail in the short space at my disposal so I will attempt to answer a few questions which may be stirring in your minds when you think of the future and especialy the problem of Post-War Housing in your own locality.

Here are the questions:–

1. What kind of house will be built by the Rural District Council after the war?
2. Will it be like Laundry Cottages or Dodford Lane?
3. How much rent will I have to pay and are the rates included?
4. How do I become a Council Tenant?
5. Who is responsible for repairs?

The answer to all these questions can be summed up in the well known slogan – 'It all depends on you'.

The Rural District Council can borrow money from the Government and raise the rest of the necessary expenditure on building and purchase of land by an extra rate and by Housing

Loans. Before the war all Local Authorities built houses under this scheme. Generally the houses were designed by an architect employed by the Council or they (the Council) would decide to build according to one of the standard types of so called Council Houses which designs were put forward by the Ministry of Health. Your Local Councillor should be able to tell you how the houses in Dodford Lane and Laundry Cottages came into being as he is your representative on all matters relating to the Welfare of Girton residents on the Rural District Council. Each Local Authority has a Housing Committee who authorises the architect, study the layout and plans and pass them when satisfied, consider the estimates and costs and instruct the contractor to do the building. The work of this Committee is brought before the full Council who give the final word to go on with the job. It is up to you to see that your Local representative is fully conversant with what the electors in the village require. There is every reason to believe that beauty and efficiency can be combined and that houses in every village can be built in keeping with local contour. This has been done in Madingley and Grantchester and could be done just as well in Girton.

Council houses are not always let at an economic rent. (If one considers an economic rent as the rent which will cover the repayment of money borrowed and cost of maintenance and management.) The Government had paid grant up to £9 per annum per house for forty years to supplement the income which meets such costs. The remainder of the balance required is raised, as previously stated by local rates. If you study the Demand note for Rates sent out by the Rural District Council you will see how much is raised that way for Housing in the District. Before the war the lowest Economic Rent on a house costing about £500 would have been approximately 12/– to 15/– per week including rates. This amount was in many cases too great a slice out of the family income so the house was let at 8/– to 10/– per week (including rates) and the balance made up as explained previously.

Every Authority has a list of Housing Applicants and anyone can 'put their name down'. All applicants fill in a form stating composition of family, district preferred and so on. It is usual to take that list in strict order and as your name comes to the top of the list you are offered a house. In addition to this list, under the Housing Act 1936 Local Authorities are obliged to give reasonable preference to 'persons who are occupying insanitary or overcrowded houses, have large families or are living under unsatisfactory housing conditions.'

All dwellings of the type stated above are the entire responsibility of the landlord regarding repairs, though every tenant is expected to co-operate to the best of his or her ability.

These are the general rules of yesterday and today but the whole subject of Housing is under review. The demand for housing accommodation is tremendous and the immediate problem after the war will be to find houses for those young married couples who have never had a home of their own, and also for those who have been rendered homeless by enemy action. Plans for temporary dwellings are being prepared. It is expected that the Government will give each Authority power to proceed at the earliest possible moment and then it is up to them to see that the job is done well and the housing applicants satisfied.

E.E.

Post-War Council Houses in Pepys Way

6 Church Lane,
Girton.
May 1944

Dear

The village is now looking delightful. The drab greys and browns of winter have gradually been replaced by the fresh green of the hedges and trees and the bright colours of the spring flowers; it is amazing what a changed outlook one has on life when the weather is sunny and the countryside is bright and cheerful. The copse at Girton College has been beautiful this year; first there were masses of snowdrops, then came the crocuses, and now it is a blaze of 'dancing' daffodils.

If you could have visited our village during the past week you would have seen notices announcing that the Annual Parish Meeting is to be held in the Institute on Wednesday at 8pm. In this country we try, at any rate in peace time, to rule by democratic principles; the Parish Council is the lowest but not the least important of our governing bodies. The present Girton Parish Council under the chairmanship of Mr M.S. Pease has made the villagers really conscious of their duty and obligations to their village and each other. We have been most fortunate in having such a capable chairman; under his guidance the Parish Council has, since it took office in 1937, been responsible for many improvements in the village, these include water, lighting, more frequent collection of unburnable rubbish and much tidying up, such as filling the pond at the entrance of the Rec, planting the tree, providing a seat on the Green, and the removal of the Posters from the Smithy. These are but a few of the improvements which spring to my mind as I write, many of you I'm sure can recall others. One rather interesting task undertaken by the Parish Council was that of extending the Parish Boundary, few parishes have made use of this ancient privilege, in our case it became necessary as quite a number of houses in the village were in the Histon Parish; when our boundary was extended to the brook this anomaly was removed. In addition to this 'material' work the Council does a great deal of advisory work which never reaches the ear of the general public; they also provide representatives for such bodies as the School Managers and the Trustees of the Village Institute.

Since 1928 Mr Pease has been a well-known member of the Chesterton R.D.C., and during the past year has been its Vice-

Chairman; the knowledge of his ability in local government matters has extended far beyond our own area, and some years ago he gave evidence before a Royal Commission on Local Government. While on this subject we must not forget that Mr Pease is supported by his most capable and energetic wife who is our County Council representative and a J.P. It has been mine, and I'm sure your experience, that whenever you seek advice or help you can rest assured that 'Reynolds Close' will provide not only sound advice but a warm welcome whether you go early or late.

And now to the Annual Parish Meeting; this year it proved so interesting, and so many people wished to air their views that at a late hour the meeting had to be adjourned and altogether five hours were spent in discussing Parish affairs! I hope to report the meeting to you, for not only was it an interesting review of the Parish Council's work, but also of the various other organisations in the village. Obviously I cannot give a detailed account of the $5\frac{1}{2}$ hours of report and discussion in one N.L., and I shall for the next month or so deal with various sections of the meeting so you may get what I hope will be a picture of your village in War and its hopes for the coming peace.

The Meeting was well attended and it was opened by our new Clerk, Mr C.E. Lintott, reading the minutes of the previous meeting; after these had been confirmed the Chairman recalled the great loss sustained by the Parish and the Council through the death of Miss Hibbert-Ware. 'No words of mine' continued the Chairman, 'could convey to you what the loss of so gracious a lady has meant to the Council and the village'. At this, the meeting was asked to rise and stand for a few moments as a mark of respect to the memory of Miss Hibbert-Ware.

In his report of the Parish Council the Chairman pointed out that as elections were in abeyance during wartime it was the policy of the Council to elect as far as possible a new member of the same type and outlook as the one who had just vacated the seat. He had much pleasure in announcing that the Council had elected Mrs H.W. Leakey to fill the vacancy caused by the death of Miss Hibbert-Ware.

Life had been 'hum-drum' in the village, but the high-light of the year was one evening – as already reported in the N.L. – when the Council was meeting, the capitulation of Italy was announced and the Council immediately telegraphed the congratulations of the village to the Prime Minister, and in due course received the official thanks. During the year the Council had to repair again the pavilion on the Rec, and they also removed two unsafe elm trees from the entrance to the Rec; we are glad to say that their removal has in no way affected the pleasant entrance. Correspondence was entered into with the Histon Parish Council with regard to the repairing of the Girton-Histon footpath which resulted in getting something done, if not quite to our satisfaction.

After the accounts of the Parish Council and the statement of the Parochial accounts were agreed to without dissent the meeting moved to Item 4 on the agenda, namely to receive the Report of the School Managers. This report caused a great deal of discussion as so many people felt strongly that now was the time with the new Education Bill before Parliament, that we in Girton should change from an Endowed school to a completely controlled Council School. Our school building which is 100 years old is out of date, it requires rebuilding, the sanitary arrangements were described as 'shocking' and should receive immediate attention. Others wanted to know what provision will be made for the 51 children under 5 who live in Thornton Road? This school question is so complex and important that I have asked Mr Booth, Headmaster of Littleton House School, to write about the New Education Bill.

We must leave the Parish Meeting now for news in brief:–

Congratulations to our Village H.G., they represented their Company in a Battalion competition, they won this and have now succeeded in gaining a place in the final of the District Competition (Cambs. & Norfolk) which will take place in the near future.

News has been received from Arthur Evans who has arrived safely in India; his father told me that he himself celebrated his majority in that country during the last war, and it looks as though Arthur will do the same. Bob Coe has arrived in East Africa and 'Jack' Asplin is at Freetown, Sierra Leone. Maurice Songer has been transferred from the

Bob Coe, R.A.

Middle East to Basra. 'Gummy' Naylor has been home on Foreign Service leave.

Only one letter has been received during the past month by the N.L. It came from John Chapman who said 'I am well and send greetings to all my pals'. An airgraph from Stan Dixon says he has successfully completed his pilot's course and expects to arrive in this country in the near future.

Miss Joan Baker, who many of you will recall as an assistant mistress at our local school was married during the Easter holidays to Lt. Clarke, to them the N.L. sends congratulations and best wishes.

May I recommend two small books which I'm sure will interest you; one called *The Countryman's College* by H.C. Dent and published by Isaac Pitman, price 1/–. It describes the Village College at Impington and gives a description of the type of training our children receive. There are many views of the College, and you will see photographs of Mr Pease, Miss Hibbert-Ware and some of our own village children. The other booklet is called *Escape at Dawn* by Miss (Frida) Stewart, published by Everybody's Books, price 2/–. Miss Stewart is the daughter of Mrs H.F. Stewart of Girton Gate who is well known for her work in the village, especially for the Women's Institute. These books are well worth reading and if you get your folks at home to send you them they will bring to you a breath of the village.

That's all for this month; try and keep this letter so you will be able to follow the next exciting instalment of the Parish Meeting!

Lots of luck and best wishes,
Yours sincerely,
F.C. Barrett.

POSTSCRIPT

The Education Bill is progressing favourably from stage to stage and should soon become the Education Act. There are limitations to the Bill, but like everything else, perfection cannot be attained at a single stroke. It is to be regretted that a date for the raising of the school leaving age to 16 could not be fixed, for without equality of leaving age there can be no equality between secondary schools. The system of fee-paying in such schools is to remain, and with this system again there can be no equality between those schools. There is no clause in the Bill which will ensure reduction in the size of classes in all types of school. Without that fundamental reform there can be no real equality between school and school, between stage and stage, between primary and secondary. There is apparently necessity for compromise on the dual system. Without drastic improvement in the whole fabric of our rural schools there can be no equality between town and country. Without a modification of the system of ungenerous and inequitable grants to local education authorities there can be no equality between area and area, but with all its limitations the Bill is a great step forward to a democratic system of education. It embodies a new and worthier conception of the value and purpose of education. The Act of 1921 defines the duty of the parent in these words; 'to cause that child to receive elementary instruction in reading, writing, and arithmetic'.

The Bill of 1944 abolishes the term 'elementary' and goes on to provide that: 'The statutory system of education shall be organised in three progressive stages to be known as primary education, secondary education, and further education; and it shall be the duty of the local education authority for every area, so far as their powers extend, to contribute towards the moral, mental and physical development of the community by securing that efficient education throughout those stages shall be available to meet the needs of the population of their area.' The Bill does indeed provide a magnificent opportunity – a framework within which we can build an educational edifice of which we may be proud. But we must help the builders. We must have faith and confidence in our cause because the youth of our country is its finest asset.

The Old Rectory, at this time the home of Littleton House School

The Prime Minister has said in a broadcast to the nation that 'the people have been rendered conscious that they are coming into their inheritance'. But to you, wherever you may be, the term 'people' will assume a much more personal cloak. 'The people' to you will mean those you have left in your own home, in your own village. Have they been rendered conscious that they are coming into their inheritance?

Whilst serving with H.M. Forces I was humbly thankful to see that these 'home' questions, these questions from which the men were temporarily divorced but in which they would have a vital interest on their return to normal life, were not pushed on to a shelf as something of no immediate concern. On the contrary, these questions were discussed in the full realisation that there was nothing of greater importance, and it is this spirit which pervades Girton on the question of our future education. Girton is a strong community already, but it will go from strength to strength because of the strength of its people, because of the awareness of a great part to be played. Girton will grow and there will be need for increased accommodation in its schools. There is a demand for a modern school building. There is a demand for a modern building in a more suitably placed situation. It is realised that Girton holds an important place on the outskirts of a famous borough. It cannot afford to lag behind in the amenities it will offer to its children. Those of you who have been away for some time will be grateful for the watch being kept over the welfare of the youngsters. This enthusiasm is grand and is something of which we might be proud. It is sweeping through the village like flood waters, but like flood waters it will need control if we are to reap its maximum benefit. This energy will not be allowed to die. For the benefit of our children it must go on, and should go on through channels which will give it weight and power. We need to have certain facts, we need to know the child population of the village today, we need to know the approximate school population of the village in 5 years' time, and in 10 years' time. We need to know in which area the children live, and in which areas others are likely to live. When these facts are obtained they can be placed before the responsible authorities in a spirit of co-operation, and these same authorities will be grateful that the people of the village are doing their utmost to help them in the great days of re-organisation which lie immediately ahead.

W.B.

6 Church Lane,
Girton.
June 1944

Dear

To you so far away, does the phrase 'Girton in June' convey to you thoughts of home, family and friends, does it bring before your mind's eye pictures of High Street, Duck End, Woody Green; of fields and trees, of the Rec beside the Church; does it recall lying in the shade and drowsily hearing the crack of the cricket ball as it is driven from the wicket to record a mighty sound when its flight is terminated against the corrugated iron building which we call the pavilion? What is our village like now? There is no cricket, but the trees still provide the shade from the waxing sun – this spring we have had lots of sunshine – the south wind still wafts the scent of roses and hedgerow flowers into the lanes and byways; and only today I watched a mother thrush pushing portions of a fat worm, gathered from my lawn into the mouths of her two vocal offspring. The winter wheat is well established, how pleasant it is to walk along the footpaths from Duck End to the Huntingdon Road, and watch the wind bending the young shoots as it chases across the fields, creating almost every shade of green in the wake of its sprightly gallop. In the large field opposite the laundry sugar beet has been drilled. When the drilling was complete the field was ridge-rolled and the motive-power was changed from a caterpillar tractor to two fine Percheron horses. But this you will say is Girton I knew in peace time, is it really unchanged by the hand of war? If you could walk through our streets in the early morning you would see the navy blue clad Wardens and First-Aid men returning home after keeping watch during the night, the birds' song to greet the morn would probably be drowned by the sound of massed bombers leaving vapour trails behind them as they go forth on their destructive errand. Strange it may seem, but we find ourselves doing as we did during the 'Battle of Britain', only this time in reverse, that of counting the planes as they depart and again on their return. We do not need the B.B.C. to tell us that our planes have been over enemy territory, we have already watched their going and have noted the returning, battle-scarred planes, making a proud, if noisy, effort to keep in formation with their more fortunate fellows. Later in the day the bus comes to the village to take the workers to the town, our bus is now propelled by Producer gas which is made in a strange contraption attached to the rear of the bus; while this machine saves petrol it is not reliable, and consequently the bus does not always run according to the time-table. Days pass quickly, sometimes we have the pleasure of meeting men home on leave, only a few minutes chat, however, as there is work to be done; our evenings are filled with meetings, Civil Defence, Home Guard, etc., till finally when day is almost done and we are thinking either of bed or our turn of duty, we hear the distant roar of the night bombers as they soar into the sky and as we take a last look at the setting sun we wish the now silhouetted planes a safe return and 'happy landing'. Our sleep is disturbed, all night long the roar continues and it is only with the coming of a new day that peace reigns for a short spell. This is but a glimpse of your village in June 1944. Space does not allow a more detailed description. I know that you would like to hear how your people are faring but I feel incapable of painting a true picture of them here at home, of their faith and hope and bearing, another more capable than I must write. And now may I return you to the Annual Parish Meeting and by the way my attention has been drawn to the statement in last month's N.L. 'that our school is 100 years ... old and the sanitary arrangements were described as shocking', it was felt that unless this statement was qualified it might convey the impression that the school lavatories were injurious to health. This thought was never implied by the word 'arrangements' and as the chairman pointed out the question of cleanliness was not under discussion, the L.E.A. and the School managers are quite satisfied from that point of view. What did shock the people however was that the primitive bucket system operates at the school, while they have for the past eight or nine years had flush lavatories in their houses here in the village. Our Chairman further pointed out that nothing could be done to alter this primitive system, as the school does not possess sufficient land on which to build a cesspool and septic tank, even if such work could be done at this juncture of the war. We all hope that immediately after the war a sewer will be laid throughout the village, and then difficulties such as this will be quickly solved.

Following the School Manager's Report I had, as Youth Organiser, pleasure in giving an account of Youth activities in the village and the County which is administered by 'The Service of Youth' Dept, of the Cambridgeshire Education Committee. You have already heard something of this work in earlier N.L.'s and as many interesting developments are taking place I propose, therefore, to write a postscript about them at some future date.

Salvage was not without problems

The next item on the agenda was to receive the Salvage Accounts. The Clerk, who is the Salvage Officer for the village, reported that approximately 9 tons of paper, $\frac{1}{2}$ ton of bones and 2 cwts of rags and scrap iron had been collected during the past year; from the proceeds of the sale £36.8.3. had been received; after grants had been given to the Girton Forces Fund, the Nurses Association, etc., a balance of £18.8.0. was carried forward, making a grand total of £90.2.11. in the bank. Various questions regarding the collection of salvage were raised by the meeting and Mrs Green produced a lighter touch when she asked 'Cannot a bye-law be passed to stop the dogs of Girton stealing from the receptacles bones which had been placed there for salvage?' It was agreed that such a law might be passed, but the dogs of Girton are no respectors of bye-laws! However, Mrs Green was promised a substantial dustbin which would prevent her losing her bones! The salvage of bones in Girton has always amused me, I feel the organisers have a sense of humour; you must have noticed the little boxes throughout the village which display a notice on which is written 'Women of Girton put your bones here' and again outside the First-Aid Post a large dustbin with the word 'Bones' written across it!

The meeting now moved from Salvage matters to Accounts of the Town Charity and then to Accounts of the Village Institute, without dissent. At this point Mr J.H. Garner, Chairman of the Entertainment Committee stepped forward to give an account of his stewardship. In his opening remarks he stated 'Although I as Chairman receive many thanks for our work on behalf of our serving men and women, I feel that no Chairman was ever supported by such a loyal and energetic committee, and I now ask those organisations which elected representatives to this committee if they would agree to the same members serving for another year'. Mr Garner also asked on behalf of his committee that permission be granted to start a reserve fund so that when our serving men and women did return home we will be able to welcome them this time in a fitting manner. The accounts showed that during the past year £122 had been raised by means of socials, whist-drives, Dances, donations etc., making a total of £159 at the bank, of this amount £73.18.0. had been distributed to the Forces, £28.8.0. transferred to the Prisoners of War account and after the various expenses had been settled left a balance in hand of £31.0.0. Again we must leave the Parish Meeting. Next month I hope to tell you about Girton's proposed Post-War plans, and also try to give you details of the proposed memorial to Miss Hibbert-Ware.

And now for news in brief:–
Congratulations Girton Home Guard. They have proved themselves in open competition to be by far – the nearest platoon was 21 points behind – the best battle platoon in the district. The district comprised the counties of Cambs, East & West Norfolk, and the Isle of Ely. You must all agree that is indeed a creditable performance.

The village is energetically preparing to 'Salute the Soldier' concerts, dances, whist drives, and a fancy dress parade have all been arranged.

On Saturday, May 20th, it is proposed to hold an Empire Youth Sports Rally on Cambridge Town Football Ground. The object of the Rally is to introduce the symbolism of Commonwealth of Nations in a way which will appeal to young people and at the same time stimulate physical fitness. There will be six teams from the County and two from the Borough, each representing a Dominion or other unit of the British Commonwealth and the events are to be decided on the team principle. No individual prizes will be awarded, but the winning team will receive from Lord Huntingfield a Laurel wreath shaped in the Victory V. George Seymour, Ken Hancock, Lawrence Evans and Betty Amps have been chosen from our village to represent the Impington Area in various events.

Letters have been received from Tom Pauley, John Chapman and Kathleen Parfitt, to you all many thanks, I hope to reply later. Jack Collings has arrived in Ceylon.

That's all for this month, all our best wishes and kind regards
Yours sincerely,
F.C. Barrett.

POSTSCRIPT

Since writing this N.L. I have heard with deep sorrow and regret that Tom Pauley has died in a Middle East Hospital as a result of an old wound.

Tom, a most likeable lad, and a fine sportsman, received shrapnel wounds in the head and back during the battle of El Alamein, and although we knew he was to have another operation on his head, he appeared to make a good recovery.

N.L. readers will recall how on leaving hospital he was trained as a cook and on completion of this course he was detailed for a more advanced course, whether he actually went on this I do not know, but in a letter which I received a few days ago he told me that he was transferred to mountainous country. His final words were 'If there are any village lads in any fighting just now I wish them the best of luck'.

Tom Pauley, R.A.S.C.

We feel particularly sad at Tom's death, he lost his father in the last war, and his mother died soon afterwards, he and his two brothers were brought up by their aunt, Mrs E. King.

To his wife, and his son and daughter, both of whom are under four years of age, we send our sincere sympathy.

This evening, as this letter is going to press, I have heard with deep regret that Cyril 'Son' Wilson has been killed on the Burma front. At the moment news is scant, but I hope to have further details next month.

F.C.B.

6 Church Lane,
Girton.
July 1944

Dear

For the great event of June 6th there is no precedent in history. Never has so vast a world held its breath in eager suspense waiting for news of the landing army. Four years ago a small British force took ships from Dunkirk beaches leaving behind it nothing but a ghostlike memory, but taking with it the spirit that was to sustain the courage of Europe. There followed four long, weary years in which everyone toiled and sweated for this day, the day of liberation not only of Europe but liberation for ourselves in order that we too may live our lives in our own particular way. You have read your newspapers, and heard on the radio how it happened and how it has progressed, but how was the news received in Girton? Those who had to be at work by 8 o'clock did not hear the B.B.C. announcements, but those who went later, when they had recovered their composure gathered in little knots in the road talking about the situation. Others could be seen cycling to work eagerly discussing possible moves. Throughout the day we listened to the official announcements on the radio and as we rushed past the news vendor's stand in Cambridge on the way home, it displayed the notice 'sold out', because of this we felt glad that we were one of 'Albert's' regulars and would be able to read the latest news when we got home. During the evening while a service of intercession was held in the Church, I was delivering the N.L. to your homes, and it took sometime to realise that your people's attendance at Church was the reason why there was no response to my repeated knocking. I met the congregation as I came down the street, it was composed mainly of women, your wives, mothers and sweethearts, they had been to pray, not only for success of our arms, but especially for you, whether you were in the invasion, Italy, or Burma, they were solemn and quiet. They did not, as they do usually, stop and tell me with pride of your doings. I feel their thoughts were not, 'Will success attend your arms?' – That is a forgone conclusion – rather they felt that you had gone perhaps to the greatest task yet committed to your doing. It seemed strangely difficult to comprehend this immense happening, though it is so near to our homes; it seems so much bigger than anything we have ever lived through before. When one thinks of it all, it is usually centred around the person one knows and loves and although last month I said I could not describe your people here at home, I now venture to suggest that their thoughts on this day were that they wished they could capture your strength, sureness, modesty and right, and be beside you, for it is empty here where we can only work and wait anxiously.

And now to the happenings of the month. The main feature has been the united effort by the village to 'Salute the Soldier'. The week's events opened unofficially on Saturday evening when a fancy dress social was held for the children. The costume which gained first prize was indeed appropriate for this crucial hour, was worn by Barry Hales, who had on a brown boiler suit to which had been sewn a great many 'dead' matches, and around his head and on his belt was the slogan 'No more strikes, Salute the Soldier'. On Sunday, a windy and bitterly cold day, we had a parade through the village by the Civil Defence units and an interesting demonstration by the Home Guard. During the evening a concert was held before an appreciative audience in the Village Institute.

Girton Follies, 1944

This concert was organised by the Entertainment Committee as were the events held in the village during the week. We have had several concerts on Sunday evenings recently, they have been thoroughly enjoyed by many people and it is hoped that they will be continued after the War. The decorated cycle and pram parade was headed by the drum and bugle band of the 7th Btn. Cadet Force. Tuesday was devoted to an exhibition by the school children of their handiwork and natural history specimens; a miniature post office was set up in the school and the children sold no less than £240 worth of saving certificates and stamps. A concert was given on Wed. and Thurs. evenings by 'Salute the Soldier Follies', this concert party was composed of our own village children and it was produced and directed by Mrs Miller and Mr J. Ison. The concert was a great success, and it drew a packed house on both occasions, and after paying all expenses made a profit of £21. On Whit-Monday £16 was distributed for prizes in the form of saving certificates and stamps when sports were held on the Recreation Ground for the children, and the remaining profits from the week's events were placed to the account of the Girton Forces Fund.

Girton was required to obtain £8000 in order to 'Salute the Soldier' and as a result of the week's activities and saving a grand total of £12,200 was obtained, that you will agree is indeed a creditable performance, and many people are to be thanked for all the hard work put into this effort.

On all sides we are hearing about post-war planning in Parliament and Town Councils and it seems that almost every Parish Council has plans for the future. Why is it that during a war people plan with such vigour? I think the main reason is that we are all appalled at the energy which is put purely to destructive ends and we all feel that if the same energy, money and thought were put into peaceful pursuits how much better it would be for us all. We in Girton have been told by our Parish Council of their proposals and plans for after the war. At the last Annual Parish meeting a Reconstruction Committee was formed and during the past month I have received a notice to attend the first meeting of the committee on Tuesday June 5th. You already know what happened on that day, and as the majority of the members of this committee were Civil Defence personnel it was decided to postpone it until things were more settled. Before discussing the proposals for post-war planning for the village I do hope that you folks who are in all parts of the world will keep your eyes and ears open and notice how other villages are planned and run, and we shall welcome your ideas and suggestions, for we feel that you who are in all parts of the world will have important and valuable contributions to make to our village community. And now for the Girton proposals, from my agenda I notice that it is proposed to appoint sub-committees for: (1) the Housing problem of the village, and to gather whatever evidence is necessary to press the matter upon proper Authority. (2) To survey the possibilities of a New Village Institute to include a Community Health Centre. (3) To prepare plans and suggestions for improvement of the Village Green and open spaces and children's amusement apparatus and the possibility of co-opting the Church Council regarding the replacement of some sort of enclosure for the Church Yard. Mr G. Lilley, Vice-chairman of the Parish Council, did give us a broad outline of the proposals at the Parish meeting, and I will try and tell you about them in the agenda order.

Immediately after the war the demand for houses in our village will become an acute and urgent problem, at the moment every house seems to be occupied by two families. This state of affairs is not good enough, especially when the two families have children. It has been suggested that the field at the bottom of Pepys Way be purchased and a group of council houses be built there. Our chairman has already promised that he will do his best to see that when the houses are built they will look attractive and be in keeping with our village surroundings.

With regard to the Village Institute you will recall the proposals which were made just before the war to enlarge the Institute, to install shower baths and build on to the end changing rooms so that when visiting teams came to the village we could entertain them in a fitting manner.

Girton Village Institute

We have been handicapped in our efforts to raise money for our Forces Fund because of the limited accommodation in the Institute, during the past 'Salute the Soldier Week' we had to repeat the concert for we could not accommodate at one time all the people who wished to see it, and again with the high price now-charged for a dance band we find that we have to have the Hall filled to suffocation in order to make a profit. A further point has arisen recently, that of staging plays in the Hall. At present the Hall is unlicensed and a licence will only be obtained with the greatest difficulty owing to the thatch roof, and the preponderance of wood in the building. The furniture in the Hall hardly exists at the moment and we have to rely on the long suffering and generosity of friends who kindly loan us chairs whenever we have a concert. There are still many points which could be discussed about our present Institute but I hope I have mentioned sufficient to show how much we need a new building. Space does not permit me to discuss point three but I hope to do so next month.

My mailbag has contained some most interesting letters during the past month; letters have been received from Arthur Evans and Tom Impey in India, Robt Purkis and Sid Gawthrop in Italy, and Robt Burrows in the Azores.

Thank you all very much, I am carefully preserving them so that when you come home and we decide to write that book about the part played by the sons and daughters of Girton we shall have plenty of material to draw upon. It is interesting to notice that nearly all the letters received by the N.L. are from abroad, and I feel that the job has been worthwhile when I read that you fellows have retained each copy, carry them with you on all your travels and when you feel a little home-sick you take them out and read them over again. Arthur is well, and sends greetings to all at home and abroad. He is on the lookout for you Carlos (Griffiths). Tom says that the N.L. brings him back to the family circle of the village, and home, and sends greetings to you all. He travelled out to India with Les (Jack) Dean, and since he has arrived he has met Claude Kidman. We have a village contingent in India, in addition to the people I have mentioned Len Hales and Jack Allen are there too. Ronny Lipscombe, Jack Collings and Tom Cox of Thornton Rd, are in Ceylon. Sid is enjoying life in Italy after the desert, but still looks forward to return home to laugh and talk with his pals and play cricket on the Rec. Robert (Purkis), your letter was most interesting, I look forward to meeting you personally when you return home. I was interested to hear that your wife comes from Toft, and that you are very attached to that village. I go to Toft each week to instruct P.T. to the young men from the villages round about. I find the people, as you remark, most kind. And now Robert (Burrows), your descriptive letter about the Azores was appreciated, if I had sufficient space I would publish it for all to read, for I found it most interesting, you certainly seem to have a flair for that type of writing.

Today I heard of the first Girton man to land in France, it is our old friend Roy (Gummy) Naylor. He serves in the Marine Commandos and he has landed in France with some of the first troops. Gummy we all send you our best wishes, and remember old chap, do take care! Talking of the second front, we are inclined to think that only our men folk are involved, but I was reminded that there is another side when I was told that Dorothy Songer and Joan Mitham have been at the embarkation ports, helping to feed our men before they set forth to invade, both these girls are serving with N.A.A.F.I.

That is all for this month. Lots of luck, and best wishes.

Yours sincerely,

F.C. Barrett.

POSTSCRIPT

As briefly announced in last month's N.L. we deeply regret to have to record the death of Cyril S. Wilson who was killed in action in Burma. Cyril was the eldest son of Mr and Mrs S. Wilson of 61 Church Lane and husband of Mrs Mary Wilson of 12 Girton Road. He had a very friendly disposition and was known affectionately by all in the village as 'Son'. When I first came to Girton Cyril and Tom Pauley were members of the Girton football team, and it gave me much pleasure to see and appreciate their sterling qualities. As a gardener 'Son' worked at the Cambria Nurseries and specialised in 'Alpines', here his skill in propagating and growing this interesting class of plant was exercised to the full. To his wife, and all at 61 Church Lane, we extend our sincere sympathy.

Cyril Wilson, Durham Light Infantry

A large congregation of relatives and friends attended a Memorial Service for Tom Pauley, which was held in the Parish Church on Sunday May 21st. Mrs Pauley in a letter to me wishes to thank all the very kind friends for their many letters and expressions of sympathy. She feels that she cannot reply to you all personally, but would like you to know how much she appreciates all your kind thoughts.

F.C.B.

6 Church Lane,
Girton.
August 1944

Dear

During the last weeks I have met many people who have resided in our village for the past year or so and during our conversations the following views have been expressed: 'I consider that Girton is one of the most progressive villages I have known, its people are energetic and are awake to their responsibilities as citizens'. 'I have lived in many towns and villages up and down the country, towns and villages which ranged from the progressive to the very indifferent. But I have noticed in Girton a co-operative and spontaneous desire on the part of all to assist in planning and carrying into effect all the various improvements which are now suggested. Also I am glad to notice that generally the people of the village realise that they themselves are the all important unit, not the Government or the Parish Council, and it really matters what they as individuals think and do. They also realise that if they are to create a progressive village community they must foster the communal spirit as this is the important factor, and it would not matter a jot if the village were to be merged into a larger group, say the Cambridge borough, provided they might still maintain this spirit.' This set me thinking about our village, and as I thought about the people and all the various organisations which exist in the village, I heartily agreed with them. This has been further emphasised during the past month, when through the spontaneous desire of the inhabitants which was expressed at the Annual Parish Meeting, a new organisation has been formed to enquire into the workings of the new Education Bill. In addition, the Society is to encourage the people of Girton to take an interest in Education in its widest sense and to collect data concerning accommodation, opportunities for scholarships, the number of children likely to attend the village school in the next five years and generally collect facts, not opinions, and place these facts before the responsible authorities, who in turn will I am sure welcome them, for such facts will help to assess the needs of our future scholars.

Mr M.S. Pease in opening the Parish Meeting on June 30th inaugurating this new Society, which will be known in the future as the Girton Village Education Society said, 'There is a widespread interest in education but at the same time there is also a strong feeling that all is not right in the Education world. That we shall see changes there is no doubt but we must not expect them all to come from above, there must be efforts from the people themselves, who must make known to Authority their desires.' The Girton school managers were pleased that the promoters of this organisation had waited upon them and explained their proposals, they felt that only good would result. Mrs Armitage, who spoke on behalf of the promoters said, 'That immediately the Education Bill was passed, each local authority would be required to furnish to the Board of Education a plan of their proposed changes within six months of its passing. The New Society could assist in collecting information about the future educational requirements of our children and present these to the local authority; the fact that they would be presented by an organisation would carry more weight than if it was presented by separate individuals. Furthermore, if we desire to secure the best educational facilities for our children and if we are to get these, we too must be educated; the society proposes to conduct in conjunction with the Adult Organiser of Impington College, Mr P.C.N. Tyack, a series of talks, exhibitions and films designed with this end in view'. Many people spoke in support of the Society but again my enemy, 'space', does not allow me to give a more detailed account, what I should like you to know is that you can all rest assured that your children's educational interests are being closely guarded by a vigilant group of people.

You will recall that I discussed in last month's N.L. the postwar plans of the reconstruction committee, that committee has since met and in view of what was said at that meeting I would be grateful if I may be allowed to delay discussing the outstanding point. The chairman of the meeting, Mr M.S. Pease, made an important statement and if what he had to say could be put into effect it will be of great value to the village. I regret that I am so vague, but as soon as more details are available I shall have much pleasure in telling you.

And now for news in brief:

We are delighted to hear after $2\frac{1}{2}$ years that Reg Cullen is safe and well. His parents received a postcard from him this week saying that he is in Japanese hands.

This week 9th – 15th July, has seen the beginning of the corn harvest. As I rode along Washpit Road I felt glad and sad at the same time, as I watched the winter oats come tumbling out of the binder as it whirred round the field. I always feel that the summer is almost over when I see shocks in regular rows, but I also feel glad when I realise that food will be available for another winter.

Girton Home Guard with the Shield

At a special parade of 'C' Company, No. 1 Cambs. Btn. H.G., Major-General J.A.A. Griffin, D.S.O., presented a shield trophy to No.6 (Girton) winners of Battle Platoon Competition open to all Home Guard Units in the Norfolk and Cambridge Districts. The General said 'It was a fine achievement to win a contest open to so large a number of units which could only have been done as a result of great keenness and training, coupled with good leadership'.

On August Bank holiday Monday, the Entertainment Committee propose holding a Mammoth Fete on the Recreation Ground in order to raise funds for you folks serving with H.M. Forces. A sub-committee has been formed to organise the fete with J.R. Thompson, secretary, and J.H. Ison as his assistant, G. Lilley as treasurer with K. Hancock assisting, and myself as chairman. The ladies serving on the committee are Mrs Thompson, Mrs R. Evans and Mrs R. Nightingale. I can tell you now that we have received the whole-hearted support of every organisation in the village and provided we have a fine day success is assured.

News has been received from three more of our lads who are in Normandy, George Betson, John McDougal and Lt. Jack Wakelin. We have not had any news of John McDougal for a considerable time and we wondered where he was but it has since transpired that he was severely burnt in an accident and was detailed for eleven weeks in hospital; I hope that you are quite fit now John. To you all, the whole village unites in sending best wishes and good fortune.

We have heard too about the exploits of Sid Gawthrop in Italy, he was with the 25th Tank Brigade supporting the 1st Canadian Division which smashed the Hitler line. The Canadians were so proud of this Brigade that they have now invited them to wear the Maple leaf on their berets and to carry the same emblem on their tanks.

Letters have been received from S/Sgt. H.L. Rooke somewhere in Iraq and from Q.M.S. Stearn in the Middle East. Mr Rooke tells me that the shade temperature is now 113°, but it will soon get much hotter, however he sends greetings to all his scout group and especially to his old friend Basil Wallis. Mr Stearn, the account of your leave, so beautifully typed on six sheets of foolscap, was much appreciated. I have read it through several times and passed it on to others, and I'm sure that you are correct when you say that 'These notes will at a later date revive many happy memories in the comfort of that little spot we love: "Home", and that doubtless there will be many eager enquiries and listeners after the adventures of a "Tommy" in the Middle East.' May these enquiries soon be asked, for I know of a little chap who anxiously awaits the 'Tommy's' return.

And now to the Postscript. It gave me great pleasure when the Rev G. Hibbert-Ware consented to write, but I am very sorry to tell you that he soon is to leave our village, as he is going to stay with friends in Cambridge. We have missed the wise counsel of his sister very much and now with his departure we shall feel the blow more keenly. I am sure that you all join me in sending him our best wishes and hope that he will come and see us as often as he can.

I sincerely regret that owing to several commitments we shall be unable to write to you next month, but will try to make up in the next issue.

POSTSCRIPT

In a few days time I shall have lived 14 years in Girton. I have never before in my life spent so long a time in one place; indeed I have never before lived even half that number of years in any one of my numerous dwellings. Well, that is over, now I am leaving Girton; and it is natural that in this postscript I, who came as a stranger, should say a few words about how I have found Girton.

First, and above all, I have found it a friendly place. Never was I made to feel like an outsider, an intruder. For Girton is still a village, and villages are sometimes very close communities. May it long remain a village, but still welcome a newcomer. Often and often on a winter's morning, when it was too dark for me to recognize anybody, or to be recognised, as I stepped out to go my short way up the road, it has seemed as if every passer-by, on bicycle or on foot, gave that cheery 'Good morning' which puts one in stouter heart for the day's work.

And Girton has been a pleasant place to look at. Often that verse of the Psalms has come into my mind 'The lot is fallen unto me in a fair ground, yea, I have a goodly heritage'. The town has crept up near it; but the country is unmistakably only a step away. And there, right in the centre, at the highest point of the village (as is proper) is the old church, an authentic village church; one to look upon with pride and gratitude. Old it is, for it has stood there about 600 years, though much altered since it was first built. But think of it, too, as hallowed by prayer and by the lives of many true saints, surely, and of hundreds baptised and married in it and buried around it. But the village is much older than that, for Girton's name is in the Domesday Book of William the Conqueror's time; and Girton must almost certainly have had a church before it had this one, even if it was only of wattle and mud.

What a number of suggestive and quaint names there were in old Girton. I mean place names, not names of families. That name Howes, we still have it. There was a chapel there for some hundreds of years before King Henry VIII, somewhere near the Travellers' Rest [Pub]; and it had a chaplain. For what purpose? I guess it was that travellers might pray there before entering (or even give thanks after leaving) the dangerous area of Cambridge University and town. Some fine old names have rightly been preserved by our Parish Council. Washpit Road, where the stream might be dammed and sheep washed in the pool; some remains of the dam could still be seen when I came to Girton; Duck End, where lived the poultry keepers who at Michaelmas time used to go into Lincolnshire, buy up quantities of geese and ducks, bring them to that spot, pluck the quills out of them for the university men to use (in my time quill pens were still in use), and then fatten the unfortunate geese to be sold in Cambridge. One name we may be glad has not been preserved by our Parish Council – Bloody Lane, where it was said, a murder had been committed, and a man might be seen there after midnight walking about without his head. I hope none of you have ever seen, after closing time, anybody going about without a head. (For these and other details, I am indebted to the late Mr J.T. Osborne). Other names, now I think gone, are suggestive of olden ways: Fishpond Field; Dovehouse Close; Reed Pond; Whining Close; Sheep Lairs (for Girton had a town flock and a parish shepherd); Malting Close. But one name remains in Girton which is famous all over the United States of America. For surely it was from our Bunkers' Hill where dwelt the men whose duty it was to maintain the banks against the fen waters, that Bunker Hill in America, four miles from the American Cambridge, took its name (as I have been told it did); a name counted glorious by all Americans for the battle of Bunker Hill, the first big battle of the War of Independence. How astonished your American friends would be if you took them to Girton Corner and told them that this was the real, original Bunker's Hill! Well, this is now by Goodbye to Girton; to be followed before long by your welcome back to Girton. To which may God bring you all safely.

G. Hibbert-Ware

Duck End, Old Girton

[There was no letter for September 1944]

6 Church Lane,
Girton.
October 1944

Dear

I am writing this letter to you on Sunday September 3rd, 1944. Five years of war have passed and I am glad to say there will be in Europe no sixth anniversary. As I write, before me floods many memories of those five dramatic years. While your lightning advance goes on, sober calculation is hard as to the precise length of the war – it may be over before you read this letter – or to the character of the peace. Too many memories and too many old frustrated hopes lie across the path of the advancing columns as we at home listen to the radio and hear that the Somme, Rheims, Arras, Verdun, and Ypres have been liberated – this same soil and these same towns that saw our fathers fight the same foe and finally break him but a generation ago. The Germans are collapsing and Germany will be overthrown. The day will be won, but will the peace? Lights will go on and the bells will ring, but what of our sons? Will they, too, have to tread the same bloody route? Will the men and women of every country in Europe again have to face first the old uncertainty of liberty and livelihood and, then, a newer and still bigger threat to life itself in the Third Great War? On every hand we hear suggestions that ought to be done and what ought not to be done with Germany and her Allies. I do not wish to preach but I think for us as individuals we ought never to let ourselves become complacent and satisfied as we were before the war began. I realise that news and facts can be withheld from us by interested parties but again we must use our free votes to see that we have representatives who will work for the interest of the people. Since you have been away we have missed you – more than we can say – let there be no illusions in your mind what awaits you on your return home, the housing accommodation is acute, the sanitation problem is the same as when you went away, the school building is inadequate for present needs, and those dreams of a fine recreation ground and a new village hall are still unfulfilled. Now, may I appeal to you with all sincerity that on your return home we want your help with all the jobs that will make our village community the happy and progressive unit it promises to be. During the war a new spirit has developed in the village, a neighbourliness and unselfish willingness to work for the good of the community. Plans are being prepared and discussions are taking place – I mentioned something of these in previous N.L.s – we shall go forward with confidence knowing that you as free men were able to win the war and we do not for a moment doubt your ability to win the peace. Again, may I on behalf of the village ask you to come forward on your return with your ideas and suggestions to assist our excellent Parish Council and its various sub-committees, and other organisations who have plans and high hopes for the future? They will welcome you, and be glad of your assistance.

Talking of improvements and the beautifying of our village reminds me that I have never given you a detailed account of the proposed memorial to Miss Hibbert-Ware. A committee representative of all the activities in the parish has been formed with Mr Michael Pease as chairman, in order to draw up a scheme for a memorial and to make a public appeal for funds. At the Annual Parish Meeting in March a preliminary statement was made which met with general approval and the desire was expressed from all quarters that the committee should continue on the lines suggested. The proposal is to lay out a public garden near the village school, where so much of Miss Hibbert-Ware's time and thoughts were spent during her residence in Girton. The aim would be to make this garden easily available for all for rest and quiet; to provide plenty of seats, and some shelter from wind and rain, and should be in easy reach of the bus stop.

Clearly the scale on which this plan could be carried out would depend upon the amount of money received; this promises well, for at the last committee meeting the Treasurer reported that over £150 had already been subscribed. The committee believes that £500 would pay for the vacant plot adjoining the village green opposite the school and for the laying out of the sort of informal garden that Miss Hibbert-Ware would have liked. The committee has been fortunate to secure as honorary adviser Miss Proctor, F.L.S., F.R.H.S., the garden steward of Girton College. At the meeting already mentioned Miss Proctor submitted her aims and plan of the proposed garden which is as follows:–

1. To make an informal garden which shall be beautiful for as much of the year as possible – not merely at one season.
2. That as Miss Hibbert-Ware was specially fond of birds some of the plants chosen for this garden should provide food for wild birds and suitable nesting places.

3. That a quiet and sheltered spot should be provided for older people (children being catered for in a recreation ground elsewhere; with space for a thatched hut for sheltering in during wet weather as well as for seats for use in fine weather.
4. That the layout should be one needing the minimum of upkeep in the future and the simplest kind of upkeep.
5. That plants be chosen which will succeed in a light soil.

Miss Proctor continued: 'I suggest that these aims could be met if this garden were surrounded by a belt of flowering tees such as the better varieties of flowering crab apples and thorns with possibly some ornamental cherries also. These would provide beautiful blossom in April and May with decorative fruits liked by birds in Autumn. The Autumn foliage of some of the crab apples is also very beautiful. Inside this belt of flowering trees I suggest informal drifts of some of the wild rose species – particularly *Rosa Hugonis* – *Rosa Rugosa* hybrids, and perhaps *Rosa Moyessii*. These have a fine natural growth – require almost no pruning or other aftercare – flourish on light soils – give a wealth of lovely single blossoms from May to August with large decorative hips in Autumn which birds love. The foliage is dense and thorny enough to be a safe nesting place for birds. *Rosa Hugonis* I specially recommend. It is one of the most admired features in the garden of Girton College, being smothered with clear lemon yellow single flowers for a long time in the May term. A single bush now covers about four square yards of ground and is still growing. Other wild species give displays later in the summer in pink, crimson and white shades. If there is room it might be possible to incorporate some clumps of broom among the wild roses. Miss Hibbert-Ware was, I believe, specially fond of these. The spaces between the trees and shrubs I would sow down with grass and ultimately plant with informal drifts of daffodils and narcissi for spring display, the grass to be scythed when the bulb leaves were over. In the centre – in a *very* slight dip – I would have a gravelled or tiled space for seats allowing room for a thatched shelter if wanted later – which might be grouped round a rectangular flower bed containing dwarf single roses – there is a good dwarf Polyanthus single pink rose called Laxton "Pink Delight" which is almost never out of flower. Or other flowers could be used as long as they were not of a formal bedding type out of keeping with the rest of the garden. Lavender and rosemary would be quite suitable here as both flourish on the type of soil and are "right" in a wild garden. I do not recommend a lily pond or other water as it would breed mosquitoes – nor do I recommend a sunk garden as there will be a difficulty in draining off the rain water that would collect there.'

The Alice Hibbert-Ware Memorial Garden today

On August Bank Holiday Monday all the organisations of the village combined in a great effort to raise money for their serving men and women in H.M. Forces. The general organisation of the fete was as I explained in my last N.L. arranged by a sub-committee of the Entertainment Committee. The side shows and stalls were provided and managed by individual organisations of the village between whom there was keen rivalry as to the result of their undertakings towards the main effort. With ideal Bank Holiday weather the recreation ground looked an attractive place with a gaily decorated central arena with sideshows and stalls placed around. Soon after the fete began there was assembled one of the largest crowds ever seen at a village function. The fete was opened with sports for young and old, and following this was an open tug-of-war, which was won by stalwarts of the village under the title of 'Odds and Ends'. The great laugh of the afternoon was provided by the comic cricket match which was organised by our local Home Guard; it was a complete change to see these men taking a humorous role after their serious efforts of recent months. The crowd roared with laughter to see the antics of the ancient and modern so-called 'ladies' attempting to play cricket under a hail of exploding squibs, bags of flour and soot, jets of water, to say nothing of encumbrances such as tight skirts and other apparel worn by 'ladies'! During the interval it was a peaceful scene to see the crowd seated about the Rec enjoying their picnic teas to the sound of pleasant music. After the tea interval a dancing display was given by Miss Jean Metcalfe's Troupe, this was followed by a talent and ankle competition and the day concluded with dancing. The sideshows were many and varied; these included a rifle range (Home Guard), Puppet Races (N.F.S.), Football Skittles (Army Cadets), Treasure Hunt (Church Council), Quoits (Wardens), Bran Tubs (Red Cross) Children's Play Pen (W.I. and Infant Welfare). In addition to these efforts there was a Model Railway which provided rides for the children, bowling for the pig, fruit stall, pin-table, and a Red Cross tent; the committee was grateful to many friends and local firms for their generous support. This fete demonstrated how the whole village can work together in harmony. I personally found it most exciting on the following evening when with my colleagues we counted up the takings and found that the day had realised £123 profit.

The news has been received with great regret that Len M. Johns of 29 Pepys Way has died while on Active Service in Burma. Len had lived for a number of years in Girton, he was very popular with a wide circle of friends here and in Cambridge. To his wife and parents at 56 Hills Road we extend our sincere sympathy.

Mr and Mrs H. Sadler of High Street celebrated their Golden Wedding anniversary on Monday Sept. 4th. They have lived for 35 years in Girton, and on Monday evening a reception was held in the Village Institute to celebrate the occasion, which was attended by approximately 150 guests. We would like to associate ourselves with the warmest congratulations and good wishes of the whole village to this popular couple.

Although I am three months late with the news many of you will wish to congratulate Frank Dupont on his being commissioned in the R.A.F.

A book has been published during the past month which will be of interest to a great many of you. It has been written by Alan Bloom of Oakington, and is called *The Farm in the Fens*. It tells the story of the reclamation of the long neglected Adventurer's Fen – a notable achievement which attracted widespread attention and brought the King and Queen, as well as the Minister of Agriculture on a tour of inspection. It is a grand story Mr Bloom has to tell, and he tells it extraordinarily well in 28 short chapters, which many of you will find as enthralling as a novel. If you wish to read about local men and their enterprise you ought to purchase this excellent book published by Faber & Faber at half a guinea.

Letters have been received from quite a number of serving men during the last few months. The first one came from Harry Cranfield, somewhere in France. He arrived in France within a week of D-Day and was soon at work, while, as he says, 'I am glad to be able to do my bit, but like Sid Gawthrop and Tom Impey, I'll be glad to have the opportunity to play football or cricket on the Rec once more'. To all his pals Harry sends greetings and best wishes. The next letter came from Miss K. Parfitt, she says 'that she looks forward to the N.L. and when she has read it she sends it to her brother-in-law in India, who in turn is linked with home.' Miss Parfitt in common with every letter the N.L. has received expresses great sorrow and regret on hearing of the death of Tom Pauley and Cyril Wilson. A very long and interesting letter was received from Les Impey in Italy. Les, your kind remarks about the N.L. have more than repaid me for my trouble and I am passing your letter on to Miss Wallis who as you already know types and duplicates the N.L. Your points about the Portal House have been noted and I have passed your remarks on to a member of our Housing Committee. Les asks that greetings and best wishes

Tom Impey, R.E.

be sent to all his pals 'especially to my brother and Len Hales in India'; then he adds this significant sentence – I don't quite understand what he means! 'Tell Len I shall "sting" him for a pint down at the George when this is all over and that goes for brother Tom as well!' Les, I did enjoy your letter. The next letter was received from Sgt. Durham, he is serving with a Searchlight Battery and has seen a great deal of successful action against the Doodle-bugs. Congratulations on your efforts, we admire your good work. I'll do everything in my power to try and get you a wireless set – I have been asking all my friends, so far without success, but don't give up hope yet. The last letter came from John Chapman who is with a heavy Ack Ack Battery. John, your regular letter is always welcome; I shall get Jack Collings' address for you and attach it to your N.L.

Finally, may I appeal to those of you who have been receiving the N.L. for over a year and have never written. You are interested to hear about others, they want to hear about you – come on, do try and find time to drop that oft-intended line.

As I conclude this letter news has been received from Arthur Evans who says that he has been evacuated by air from Burma to India, suffering from jaundice and suspected fever. I hope by now, Arthur, you are fit and well again. That is all for this month except to wish you good lack and God speed,
Yours sincerely,
F.C. Barrett.

6 Church Lane,
Girton.
November 1944

Dear

I think you must have noticed that I am always a month in arrears with news and descriptions of our village; the reason for this is that it takes about a month to collect the news, write and duplicate the letter. I am told that to you in distant parts time is of no consequence and that news of the village is always welcome, but to you at home the news maybe a bit stale. For instance, I may describe what the village looks like at a particular season but by the time you receive the letter quite different conditions may be prevailing; so if at any time I say it is warm and sunny here and by the time you receive the letter it is snowing, please forgive me – you'll know the reason.

Well, here we are in October. Can you imagine what the village looks like just now? The leaves on the trees are turning from green to gold and lemon before they float quietly to the ground, and the fields of bare stubble lie silvery under the autumn sun. The stackyards of the village farms are full again and threshing tackle is drawn in among the stacks, and the engine chimney is breathing a gentle whisp of blue-grey smoke. Today is Sunday – I always seem to write to you on the Sabbath; I think most of your people do the same – and this evening I heard the church bells ringing out from several churches within hearing, and as I write I think of all the people in those villages making their way by road, lane, and footpath to the little churches among the lime trees for the Harvest Festival. I'm not a churchgoer, but I was brought up to Church of England rites and I have always felt that the Harvest Festival service was a lovely symbol. Even to churchgoers I think there is more in the Harvest service than just the fact that it is a church service. Harvest rites go back into the bone and fibre of mankind long before Christianity, long before history even. I have been chatting with Mr Searle and he told me very sadly

'Threshing tackle ... among the stacks'

that the harvest this year was only average. He also told me very sadly that he had a wonderful field of wheat along the Oakington Road and just when he was about to cut it someone – probably a tramp – set it on fire, and the whole lot was burnt; this was indeed a loss.

Do you recall that I discussed in the August N.L. the Post-War plans of the Reconstruction Committee? I mentioned that the Committee had met but I was not in a position to discuss publicly the plans of the proposed Community Centre. Mr M.S. Pease, the Chairman, invited Mr Henry Morris, Director of Education for Cambridgeshire, to meet the Committee, and the possibilities of a Community Centre for Girton were discussed. At the conclusion of the meeting Mr Morris asked that the various points which had been raised during the discussion should be recorded and sent to him for his further consideration in the form of a letter. Again I am indebted to our Chairman for allowing me to publish his letter to Mr Morris; I shall not comment on it in this N.L., but I do ask you to give it your most careful consideration, and send any comments or suggestions to the Chairman or myself and we shall study them carefully.

Copy of letter

Reynold's Close
Girton.
9.9.44

Dear Morris,

Thank you for your note of August 10th about the suggested Community Centre for Girton, which was discussed at the meeting which you attended here on July 31st. The idea at the moment is to make a plan for a centre which will eventually include:–

A new School.
The Recreation Ground.
Sports Pavilion, changing rooms, and baths.
An Assembly Hall and canteen.
An Infant Welfare Centre, Antenatal Clinic and day Nursery
Room for Adult and Youth activities.
Library and Reading room.
Gymnasium.

As far as the County Council is concerned, the essential question at the moment is the need for a new school in Girton. A careful house-to-house survey of infants in Girton carried out in May by the Girton Village Education Society (copy enclosed) shows that the number of children reaching the age of 5 during each of the next five years 1944–1948, will be 40, 42, 35, 23, and 35. On the assumption that those over 11 will go to Impington, that makes 180 new entrants up to 1948, to which must be added 18 of the age group 10 to 11. The present school was built in 1845. Notwithstanding subsequent addition and improvements it consists of but three classrooms. By pre-war standards it could accommodate 117 children, it is true that during the last few years an extra class has been accommodated in the Village Institute. But this is obviously unsatisfactory from every point of view and could be tolerated only as a war-time stop gap measure. After the war the Institute ought to revert to its proper use as a Village Club.

As you know, the present school could not be enlarged on its present site, which is already very cramped and is unsuitable by reason of the public right of access across the school yard to the row of cottages behind. Clearly, therefore, a new junior school will have to be built in Girton as soon as building becomes possible.

The question of site, however, should be settled now. Latterly much new building has taken place at the College end of the parish and more development must be expected there. The survey of children already mentioned showed 80 children under 5 living in this new residential area at the College end and 100 in the area of the 'old village'. The population figures are therefore not decisive. The site suggested by the Girton Reconstruction Committee is shown on the enclosed plan. This would front the existing Recreation Ground. Services are available, including, it is to be hoped, sewerage. The site is Glebe land, at present used for allotments. It is the property of the Lord Chancellor, as patron of the living. The advantages of this site for the suggested school are:–

1. That sufficient land is available for the whole of the suggested Community Centre.

2. That since it adjoins the existing Recreation Ground and the present school master's house, no fresh provision need be made by the County Council for playing fields and, it is to be hoped, for the school house.

3. That no break is made with the traditional social centre of the village.

4. That on artistic grounds, the Church, the Village Green, the Recreation Ground, and the trees grouped round them provide an appropriate setting which it would be difficult to equal in the parish.

With regard to the other items suggested for the Community Centre, all that can be said at the moment is that money might well be forthcoming by way of public subscription towards the cost of the assembly hall and the pavilion. Presumably the assembly hall would be part of the school, as at Impington. But if extra expense were involved so as to make it more readily available for public use in the evenings, this extra expense should reasonably be met out of local funds. The same situation might arise with regard to the pavilion, though it is realised that in this case the education authority might prefer to put up something for the exclusive use of the school.

I hope this letter covers the points necessary for a preliminary survey. No doubt you will let me know what you think of the proposals.

Yours sincerely

M.S. Pease

And now for news in brief:

The Garden and Allotments Society held a show of garden produce in aid of the Red Cross on Sept. 9th; considering the dry season it was amazing to see such excellent exhibits. After the show the exhibits were auctioned and the sum of £11 was handed to the Red Cross. The Allotment Society also asked its members if they could give some onions to the Agricultural Red Cross fund; I asked Mr Garner, the Chairman of the Society, how the onions were coming in, and he replied '6 cwt. have been received, and more to come.'

The Education Society had an excellent meeting recently; they invited Dr Hallam, until recently Director of Education for the West Riding of Yorkshire, to speak on 'Selection of Children for Secondary Education'. The discussion which followed showed that the members were alive to the importance of secondary education for their children.

The village has managed to raise a football team; there are many fresh faces, but even though the team is young there is much enthusiasm. The Team has joined the Youth Centre league and will have the pleasure of playing teams from Histon, Cottenham, Sawston, and Cambridge – in fact, it will be almost like the old First Division days.

The other day I bumped into the Rev P.N. Palmer who was on a visit to friends in the village. He sends greetings and best wishes to you all, and he also promised to write another postscript for the N.L. in the near future.

Letters have been received from Jack Collings – somewhere in Ceylon. Jack was well at the time of writing but I have since heard from his mother that he had had a motor accident in South Africa; he recovered after a few weeks in hospital and was now convalescing. A welcome air-graph was received from L.A.C. R.J. Jaggard with the M.E.F. He says he 'looks forward to receiving the most welcome N.L. and although I don't know the lads personally I do by name now and I hope I shall run across some of them soon'. The other air-graph came from our old friend 'Gummy' Naylor. Gummy, you do get to some queer places; although you are unable to say where you are at the present we have guessed that you must be in America, India, or the Middle East!!! Gummy, your kind remarks about the N.L. are appreciated; I was touched when you said that you read the latest one through 10 times because you felt lonely far away from the shore of Britain. To all his pals – members of the football team etc. – Gummy sends best wishes and hopes to see you all soon.

Jack Collings, R.N.

I have much pleasure to include a postscript by Mr H. Bradfield in this month's N.L. Mr Bradfield is so well-known that I shall not, as it were, introduce him to you. We are all delighted that he quickly recovered from his illness and is well again.

That is all for this month.
Yours very sincerely
F.C. Barrett.

POSTSCRIPT

November, 1944

A conversation with a fellow passenger on a bus the other day set me thinking again on the human element, that important factor in the general scheme of things, which must always be taken into account. My companion, a member of the staff of a big public concern, had apparently been transferred from one administrative district to another, leaving behind a department controlled by a dominating and aggressive type of individual, highly conscious of his own importance, he had found himself in an entirely new setting, where a team of active and co-operative individuals were directed by a man of intelligence and real ability. The difference in atmosphere and general efficiency had amazed him and he had settled down happily to work as he had never done before.

Probably most of us at some time or another have seen this kind of thing, for few spheres of life are altogether free from the type of individual who must be all or nothing. How often the human element has scotched the wheels of progress when it might have increased the horsepower. Amongst many things that must concern us in the future, the question of human relations is vital. In the wider sense it is this factor that decides ultimately the turn of events. In our more intimate circles personal relationships are closely related to happiness and in community life little progress is possible where people are at 'sixes and sevens'. The war should have taught us something in the way of getting along together. Allowing for the outcroppings of human weakness here and there, it has revealed a good deal of common spirit and unselfish service. One may hope that the services will be diverted into new and useful channels. Or shall we feel that less spectacular effort to secure the peace is somehow less important than winning the war? In many ways during the war the human element has been 'tuned in' to serve the common good. In our own village for instance, community life has leapt forward with new impulse. It has become evident to most of us that the old order of things can no longer adequately serve the true interests of the village and we are facing up to some of the implications of change which the times demand.

6 Church Lane,
Girton.
December 1944

Dear

What, again December! Has another year gone by? I am always staggered when it is time to write the N.L. each month, but I am doubly staggered now that it is almost Christmas. The time has simply flown since last year, if anything I have been even busier than ever before, yet if I stop and think it has been a long tense and exciting year, a year that will go down as probably the greatest in the history of this island. We have seen the invasion of the Continent and we have no doubts that the war in Europe is almost at an end. We had high hopes that this Christmas you would be home again and around your own firesides, but that was not to be; however, there are in our village many hearts that long for your return and will be thinking of you.

At Christmas time you always think of absent friends and I thought that you would like to know where your pals are now serving. I am sorry if my list is incomplete – I apologise in advance, but it is due to the fact that some of you have not written or that I have been unable to enquire as to your whereabouts from your people when I delivered your last N.L.

As far as I can gather H. Cranfield, G. Betson, R. Evans, J. McDougal, G. Pauley, J. Wakelin, K. Deane, K. Matthews, J. Secker, R. Ellis and B. Crabb are in Holland or Belgium; T. Impey, C. Kidman, A. Evans, L. Dean,

Ken Deane, S.H.A.E.F.F.

C. Griffiths, L. Hales, J. Allen, J. Hines, V. Riley and C. Pauley are in India or Burma; L. Impey, S. Gawthrop, R.J. Jaggard, R. Purkis, S. Hankin, E.J. Stearn, R. Rooke, H. Cornell and H. Chapman are with M.E.F.; G. Huddlestone is in Canada, R. Burrows in the Azores, Bob Coe in British West Africa, R. Cole in Algiers, W. Purkis in the Bahamas, and last of all 'Gummy' Naylor I just don't know where – somewhere abroad. To those of you in Hospital, Miss J. Macalister in Cairo, Arthur Evans in India, Tom Cox in Ceylon, and Cliff Hankin here in England, I hope by the time you receive this letter you will all be feeling better.

Our thoughts also at this time are with our lads who are prisoners of war in Japanese hands, Walter Dixon, R. Cundell, C. Andrews, R.G. Austin and C. Smith. Finally, there are those who we will never forget, those who will not return, Tom (Pauley), Son (Wilson) and Len (Johns), B. (Hullyer) and R. (Gerrard). To their wives and families our hearts go out in sincere sympathy, for to them we know this cannot be a happy Christmas.

And now for news in brief. It was grand to meet Basil Wallis home on leave after three years' absence in the Middle East. He looks fit and well, but was feeling the cold. J. Asplin has arrived in England, but not home to Girton – after fourteen months in Freetown, British West Africa, and today I heard that Maurice Songer has started for home after several years in the Basra area. The Hibbert-Ware Memorial Trust have now nearly reached their objective of £500; the whole village will rejoice on hearing this news, for it is indeed a tribute to the memory of Miss Hibbert-Ware, and also the Committee who handled the appeal. I understand that work on the plot is to begin almost immediately, and if certain obstacles can be removed the Committee will be able to keep to their timetable, the details of which I have already given.

The football team has played four matches; they have won three and lost one. I have both watched and refereed their games, and – I hope they won't read this and get a swollen head – they are improving with every game.

I have been meaning to tell you that Edward (Tubby) Nightingale has been called up and is now a fully trained soldier somewhere in Wales; our latest recruit from the village is Peter

Thulbourne, he joined during the past week.

Only one letter has been received by the N.L. during the past month. It came from Lieutenant Jack Wakelin somewhere in Belgium. Jack landed in France a week after D-Day and he tells me he has been working day and night – when he did have a day's leave he was too tired to go sight-seeing in Brussels.

You will recall that last year I invited well-known village personalities to send you a Christmas greeting. I have repeated this, and hope that you may thereby feel in touch with home.

Peter Thulbourne, R.A.

Mr M.S. Pease, Chairman of the Parish Council sends greetings:–

As the war in Europe draws to its end, thinking men and women at Home are increasingly concerned about the sort of Britain to which you will return and to the sort of world in which you, and your children will live. The immediate need is houses; in comparison with this nothing else matters. Till recently it was difficult to believe that those in authority had at all grasped the size and urgency of the problem it was all too uneasily like the sorry story of weapons in the years before 1940. But today there are some signs of change in the attitude towards housing. In 1940 it was the voice of those in the services which compelled a change in the output of weapons. So today your voice is needed to join with those at home in order to give speed, drive, and fire to the work of getting ready now to build the houses for you to live in when you return. Plans for demobilisation have been made, you will get a gratuity and a suit of civilian clothes. I hope that you will put your claim on a very grateful country higher than that; a decent house and a home of your own is the least that your country can do for you. But if you want to be sure of this, you must start asking now,

and go on asking through your proper Service channels; ask for a house, not as a favour, but as your right. A right, you must remember, has always to be claimed. You make your claim, and we will see that it is heard.
Michael Pease
November 20th

Mr Garner, Headmaster of the Girton Endowed School, sends greetings:–

I greatly appreciate the opportunity given me to send a brief message to members of H.M. Forces ordinarily resident in Girton. Another Christmas draws near and our thoughts are always with you where ever you may be; everyone looks forward to your return to your homes and we appreciate to the full the enormous sacrifices you have all made on our behalf. The old village school, so well known to many of you still carries on, and with the use of the Village Institute as an additional classroom and dining room we are able to cope with any problems that happen to arise. One very pleasing feature which has been very noticeable during the five years of war is the very little effect the war has made upon the scholars (even including the evacuees), I think everyone must agree that the latter scholars were lucky indeed to be sent to Girton. The care bestowed upon them by their Girton foster-parents has borne considerable fruit in the improved physique, appearance and general wellbeing of all who have stayed with us. I must not trespass further on the limited space of this N.L. and will conclude with heartfelt good wishes from myself, staff, and scholars for a very happy time this Christmas, and a victorious homecoming for you all in the New Year.
J.H. Garner.

From a 5 year old:
Friday 10th November.
Der everyou of Girton,
I do hop yo wil cum back soon for Xmas, luv A.J.
From a 7 year old:
Dear soldiers, sailors and airmen,
I hope you win the war and then we will hang flags out of our windows when you come marching home. We will cheer you a lot. I hope there will be bananas after the war then we will buy

some if they are yellow not if they are green. They will be lovely. Yours sincerely, T.H.

From a 10 year old:

Dear soldiers, sailors and airmen,

We are writing a few lines to wish you a happy Christmas. We enjoy writing letters to you very much because we think it is very nice to have our letters go over seas, and we think it might cheer you all up a bit. We all hope that you get a nice Xmas dinner, and that you receive all the presents that are sent to you. We are getting on with the war now aren't we, and are all very proud of you – friends who are all winning it for us, and we only wish that some day we can pay you back for what you are doing for us. It will soon be 1945 now and we want to wish you good luck in the next year, and we hope that 1945 will bring you all home to us again, and this time to stay home.

S.B.

Mr Bradfield sends greetings:–

Christmas is here again and for most of us life is still very much out of gear. How attractive this milestone viewed from the heights of optimism farther back, but hope based on reality now brings the end of the war much nearer. For many of you unfortunately the mud of Holland, the Indian sun, or the uncongenial conditions of Burma must be your Christmas setting. Wherever you are may the unseen bonds of memory and affection link you strongly with those who wait for your return, and may the homeward journey of your dreams soon become reality.

H. Bradfield

The Rector sends greetings:–

I write on Remembrance Sunday, and that means it is some way ahead to Christmas, but none the less I wish you a happy Christmas, with all sincerity. This morning in the well-filled Church, members of the Home Guard, the Cadets, Red Cross and St John, the Fire Service, and other services joined with your other friends and relatives in thinking of you and praying for your success in every way. We shall of course continue to do so. In the meantime I value this opportunity of wishing you all the best and a new year of victory.

Mr Sterndale Burrows sends greetings:-

Watching and waiting still very heartiest greetings for Christmas
and the New Year come to you over the silent air, and as the poet says –

> 'Dickery, dickery, dickery dock,
> D'you hear my sentinel's chime?
> Swing, swing, you're as good as a King
> if you keep eternal time.' – The Church Clock

Mrs H.W. Leakey sends greetings:-

Peace and good will at Christmas time! For a moment during the year our hopes of Christmas leapt high and at once we found the idea of peace had widened far beyond war's end. It is to the peace of security, peace of plenty, and peace of social justice to which our minds turn in 1945. When you come home you will see our countryside with new eyes, and as I travelled the other day from Cumberland to Cambridge I tried to see what you will see – a land whose fertility is dependent on hard work, whose beauty is mainly man-made, whose people are homely, whose children are physically beautiful. Some parts of the world seem to drive straight from nature, but this, our land, is our concern; and when you come home we shall need your help in the battle of peace-making. Till then be of good heart. All Girton sends its Christmas greetings to you.
H.W. Leakey

Miss Wallis sends greetings:-

Every good wish to all serving men and women of Girton wherever they may be, and the hope that you may all very soon return safely to your families. A Happy Xmas to you all.
G. Wallis

Having completed our Christmas number it is only left for me to wish you a happy Xmas and as always good luck and God speed wherever you are.
Yours very sincerely,
F.C. Barrett.

6 Church Lane,
Girton.
January 1945

Dear

How shall I send, on behalf of the village, our New Years Greetings? Shall I just say that we wish you a happy and prosperous New Year, or shall I just say may peace and you come marching home. Mere words do not adequately convey our good wishes and our thoughts at the beginning of this New Year; to each of you in a different station, you with the B.L.A., you who are embraced by the letters C.M.F. and finally our lads with the gallant 14th Army in Burma, we would like to send an individual and personal message of hope and good cheer and tell you of our continued love and our admiration of all you are doing. May good fortune attend you and may Girton be a 'Port of Call' for you all in the near future.

The old year has died spitefully here at home. We have experienced almost every known sort of weather, fog, both valley and hill mists, which are of a different nature, sleet, drizzle, thunder rain, and just rain, frost and almost summer warmth. This infinite variety has in some measure, been disguised by the prevalence of rain, not 'Welcome blessed rain', but soggy downpours which have kept the farm workers off the fields and left the beet and potatoes in. Mr Hall did try to lift his potato crop, which he grew in the field beside the Washpit footpath. I have always wanted to be a farmer, but the sight of that field had put me off farming – at least until the spring days come round again. You may recall the field – the soil is heavy, and on the day I saw it, it was too heavy to use a spinner or any other modern device to help with the lifting, so the potatoes had to be ploughed out. As the plough went down the field the furrow which it made immediately filled with water. I felt so sorry for the people who had to lift the crop, not only was it very unpleasant work, but they had the additional difficulty of differentiating sticky clay-covered potatoes from genuine lumps of earth.

The rain, frost, warmth and shine have done more than clear the leaves from the trees. It has driven them into the ground and made skeletons of the lime and poplar leaves which had fallen earlier, the earthworms enjoy this damp dark weather, and I have noticed that on my lawn they have pulled many of these decaying leaves into their holes.

Most of you who are fortunate enough to have a copy of the Cambridge Independent Press sent to you each week will have seen in its advertisement columns notices entitled 'War Charities Act, 1940'. The notices go on to say 'That it is proposed to apply to the Cambridgeshire County Council for registration under the above act, of the X Homecoming Funds, the objects of which are shortly as follows: To raise funds for the benefit of X's men and women serving in H.M. Forces at their Homecoming etc., etc.' Many of you may have wondered why the name of every Parish which adjoins Girton has been mentioned in such advertisements, but so far not Girton's. Why? What is Girton up to? Let me say at once that the matter of a Homecoming Fund has already been discussed informally by the Parish Council and representatives of all the village organisations, and it has been decided to call a Parish Meeting on Wednesday next, December 13th. Quite a number of people have asked me why didn't the Entertainment Committee, if they represent the village organisations and activities, organise a Homecoming Fund earlier in the year? In order to answer that question, and I think it ought to be answered, I must tell you something about the work and purpose of that committee.

The Girton Entertainment Committee came into being at the request of the Village Institute Trustees who had been asked to take over the work of a previous Sports Committee whose task had been to entertain the many evacuees then resident in the village. The Trustees invited a representative from each organisation in the village to form a committee suggesting that their duty should be to raise funds for serving men and women in H.M. Forces, and to provide entertainments and sports for children resident in the village.

How has this committee fulfilled its mandate? The following figures are only part of a story of continuous enthusiasm and hard work, carried out by people who were overworked at their daily task, and in addition had Home Guard, or Civil Defence duties.

These selfsame people were also serving as active members on many other committees. However, they set to and organised concerts, whist drives, Warship week, etc., so that in 1942, '43 and '44, they were able to distribute to our serving men and women £22, £73 and £71 respectively. In addition to this £52 has been reserved for our P.O.W. return; £48 distributed in the form of entertainment for our children; £5 to wives whose husbands have been killed, £5 to Earl Haigh Fund; and 28 to the Nursing Association. The £123.10s. which you will remember was the profit from our August Bank Holiday Fete is being kept as a nucleus for a 'Welcome Home Fund', the idea being that the Committee will await the first 20 discharged men and women to return home; then invite them along with their sweethearts and wives to a do, and there officially welcome them home, the same procedure will be carried out for the next 20 returning men and so on until you have all been received back into the fold. The gifts are purely a token of our remembrance and gratitude to you for all that you are doing for us. There has never been an attempt by the committee to supplement anyone's salary with the small donations that you have received from time to time. Still you may say why didn't the Entertainment Committee start a Homecoming Fund like the other villages and provide each returning man and woman with a cash payment? There are many reasons, firstly it is outside their mandate and secondly there are many on the committee who do not agree with such payments, they think such should be a Government responsibility, and thirdly a completely new source of revenue must be tapped for we have almost reached saturation point in concerts and whist drives. However, I hope to give you full details of the Parish Meeting in my next letter, I regret I cannot attend the meeting – I have to teach an evening class that night, but I'm sure one of my good friends will report it for me. In the meantime I have written to the following villages and received from them this information. Cottenham hopes to raise £20,000 for 225 men and women, money in hand about £2,000. Histon and Impington hope to raise £20,000 for 500 serving men and women, money in hand about £2,500, Coton's target is £1,000 for 75 men and women, money in hand about £500. Now the great question is, if such sums can be raised in Girton, how is it to be distributed? Should an overseas man get the same as one who has stayed at home? Should a man who has served one year get the same as a man who has served five years? How is the residential qualification to be fulfilled? Should a married man have the same as a single man? These are only a few questions that will have to be satisfactorily answered, and I really would be grateful if you would write and tell me your point of view, for after all yours is the one that should be considered. In common with other units throughout the country the Girton Home Guard stood down a fortnight ago. Members of this platoon paraded on Parker's Piece with representatives from every unit in Cambridgeshire to receive the official 'Thank you' for services

Girton Home Guard, on parade in the Village

rendered. That was the official way, but our local Platoon had other ideas of a stand down, so Saturday 9th saw some 80 members assembling in the Village Institute for a grand Stand Down Dinner; this consisted of soup, meat rissoles, potatoes and vegetables, stewed apples and cream – Yes, real cream!! – cheese and biscuits and, need I add, a plentiful supply of beer. Here may I add that the Menu had a footnote which read Cars at 11 p.m., Wheelbarrows at midnight, Stretchers at 12.55 a.m. My reporter did not say if these were used in the right order, but I am informed that a 'good time was had by all', so much so that it was suggested that someone should shout 'as – you – were', in order that the whole thing should be repeated. I am indebted to F.A. Porter, Esq, for supplying the following note about the dinner. The guests included Major Gen. G.R. Griffin (District Commander), Lt. Col. J.M. Bryan (O/C 1st Btn.), Major H. Payne

(C. Coy. Commander), Capt. J.S. Chivers, and the following ex-members of the Platoon – Lt. Col. Mackenzie (O/C 7th Btn.), Maj. Sir F. Engledow, Lt. Swift, R.N.V.R., Capt. R. Gane, Capt. Cartwright, Lt. Dillon-Weston, Lt. Oxley, Lt. Blott, Sgt. Coe and Sgt. Matthews. After Lt. Monkman had proposed the King, Lt. J.R. Thompson proposed the Guests, and read letters of apology from Capt. Bird, who was unfortunately ill, Major Green, absent owing to Military duty and Sgt. Gerrard to whom the platoon owed so much in the early days. In reply Maj. Gen. Griffin spoke of the underlying wistfulness at the stand down, and the hardening effect the war had had on the ordinary British Citizen, who had in pre-war days adopted the philosophy of 'how much you can get out of life, not how much you can put in'. Lt. Col. J.M. Bryan and other speakers followed, interspersed with items from a volunteer concert party brought over by Mrs Pryor, which kept the audience enthralled by the jokes of Sid Walker Jun., the tap dancing of Pat and Pam and the silvery tones of Vera Walls.

And now for news in brief: It is with deep regret that I have to tell you of the sudden tragic death of George Naylor. Mr Naylor was well known in the village and the surrounding district. We should like to send his wife and family and especially 'Roy' so far away, our sincere sympathy. The football team must have read my last month's note for they have lost to Bottisham twice 3–0, lost to Cottenham after leading 3–0 until fifteen minutes from the end, 4–3; but today they have somewhat mended their evil ways by beating the Central Youth Centre 6–0. The village Education Society heard an interesting talk from Miss Preedy, advisory teacher to the Cambs. Education Committee on the Value of Parent-Teacher Associations. The Youth Centre have been holding a series of fortnightly dances in the Village Institute in order to raise money for their many activities. They hope to be able to purchase a radiogram, give a donation to their members who are serving with H.M. Forces, the Hibbert-Ware Memorial Fund and their own members' committee, which meets every two months in the Guildhall, Cambridge. I was glad to hear that Stan 'Diddley' Hankin has met Sid Gawthrop in Italy. I have little information about their meeting; but you can guess that their tongues wagged about memories of home. Two most interesting letters have been received during the past month.

The first came from Arthur Evans; Arthur, we were very worried about you when we heard that you were in hospital and had had some stitches removed. Your mother thought you had been wounded; you see your letter containing the essential information that you had been kicked on the head by a mule was delayed until after the one telling about the removal of the stitches. Your father, an old campaigner in India, of the last war, guessed what had happened and he was tickled when you said that Kitty, his old mule, was a lamb compared to the one you have. I hope that your headaches are lessening and that you are feeling better. Arthur tells me that he is in touch with Claude, Len, Ron and Carlos, but so far they have not met; he did meet Jack Dean, and to quote Arthur 'I couldn't believe my eyes'. To you all Arthur sends the seasons greetings and best wishes. The other letter came from Victor Riley. He was taking a well earned rest and was making himself comfortable with the aid of tarpaulins, bamboo poles and the inevitable pieces of string. He says 'I have four men in my "Basha" as these huts are called, and a bed made out of bamboo is to a battle weary soldier the next best thing to the Ritz'. 'This bamboo is exceedingly versatile stuff, you make huts, beds, fires, cooking pots for rice and if you are really hungry you can eat it'. Vic is in the Signals section and he says 'The little Brown Brothers, the Japs, cut our telephone wires and a sniper waits for you to come along to mend it and then shoots you'. 'I was recently slightly wounded in the head by this type of booby-trap, but in spite of an awful hair cut I will soon be presentable'. To all in Girton and Girton lads wherever they may be Victor sends greetings and his good wishes.

To you all may I again send my best wishes for the coming year, and as always, Good luck and God speed,
Yours very sincerely,
F.C. Barrett.

6 Church Lane,
Girton.
February 1945

Dear

Christmas and New Year's Day are now past. When I wrote to you last time they were still in front of me and so I could only write in anticipation, but now they are behind I can tell you something about the weather and how we here at home kept the festive season. I doubt if I shall ever forget this Christmas of 1944. It stands out with Christmas 1940, when I had been away staying with relations over the holiday, and while I was away the frost set in and the thermometer fell far below freezing point. When I returned home I was amazed and I must admit that I felt rather ashamed of myself when I saw that on the Recreation Ground a small Searchlight Unit had spent Christmas under canvas while I had been sleeping in a warm bed at night and sitting before the fire by day. Do you remember those lads? Sgt. Gill, Digger and the rest of the boys. I wonder if someone else lets them have a hot bath now, and what has happened to them? Although nature is trying hard to obliterate their hard work on the Recreation Ground every time I go there Christmas 1940 becomes again a vivid memory. However, to return to the Christmas that is just past; I never saw Girton look more lovely than in the frost and sunshine of December 25th and 26th. The previous days had been dark and miserable with cold wet fog, and also the fog of censorship regarding Rundstedt's drive through Belgium. The effect of this solid hoar frost was much finer than snow, for snow covers the fields and trees and hedges with a blanket and makes a new world; the rime revealed the ordinary world and transformed it. Every blade of grass stood straight up, a dark green with a shield of silver, dazzling and brilliant. The limes and elms against the Church waved plumes against the sky, and every branch was a magically lit Christmas tree, every twig catching the light and reflecting it.

The carol singers seemed to be more numerous this year. We had visits from several groups representing various Charities, and in the Village Institute we had a delightful Sunday evening concert given by the Corynton Trio and in this and the one organised by Mrs R. Evans we sang together 'God rest you merry, Gentlemen', 'Good King Wenceslas', and all the old familiar tunes, but in our hearts we thought of absent friends and dare we hope you will recall my last N.L., in which I told you about a Parish Meeting to discuss a Homecoming Fund. At the meeting many people expressed views for or against the Fund, but it was eventually decided by a large majority to form a Committee to raise funds for our returning men and women. Several people at the meeting suggested that instead of giving a per capita allocation it would be better to make the fund into a Friendly Society so that those returning, could if they wished, borrow money free of interest to purchase their own house or start a small business. This I must confess has many interesting possibilities, but it was eventually decided that it should be a per capita distribution irrespective of rank or length of service; at this meeting a committee numbering 25 persons was elected. This committee met on the 27th December under the provisional chairmanship of Mr M.S. Pease, to appoint persons to the necessary offices. This meeting showed once again just how busy everyone is; several people were so committed that they found it impossible to take on additional work. Mr Pease agreed to continue in the office until a permanent chairman could be appointed. Mr W. Dixon, 57 Cambridge Road, was appointed Secretary, Mr A.R. Miller appointed assistant Secretary and B.M. Turner, of Girton Corner, as Treasurer. Mr G. Nightingale, Mr H. Kidman, Mr R. Gawthrop, were appointed as Executive Committee. Various Sub-Committees were elected to organise social events, subscriptions, collections, etc. I hope to be able to tell you about the next meeting when rules and regulations will come up for approval and ratification. I wish every success to the committee. They have a gigantic task before them, and they will require the good-will and co-operation of all in the Village to make the result worthwhile.

You will recall that in a previous N.L. I published a letter from the Chairman of our Parish Council to the Cambridgeshire Education Secretary on a proposed Community Centre for our village. I was very interested to read the Government's White paper on Community Centres published this week, price 9d. it sets out to show that the idea behind the Community Centre is that neighbours can meet together on equal footing, to enjoy social, recreative, and educational activities either as members of groups following particular hobbies and pursuits or on their common needs and interests as human beings living in the same locality. As I read through this report I felt, if only we had such a place now as suggested in this report, what a boon it would be to all the various organisations and groups in the village. The Village Institute is too small for the requirements of the village. It is also most inconvenient as only one group of people can use it at a time. The demand for the use of the large room must give Mr G. Lilley a headache, it is in use every evening and now that the Homecoming Fund will require it quite a lot, there will have to be a great deal of mutual help and co-operation between the rival applicants. How much more convenient it would be if there was another room attached or if the small committee rooms were free? Those of us who have had to organise social functions can testify how the appalling lack of reasonable seats in the present building makes the organising of whist drives, concerts etc., a major undertaking, for seats have to be borrowed from and returned to Littleton House School or whoever is kind enough to loan them to us.

Among the letters which I received during the past month was one from Dick Evans, in it he recalled the farewell banquet which the Youth Centre gave in his honour before he joined the Army. He says 'When I feel a little homesick I take from my pocket the autographed menu card and recall the happy times I had at the Youth Centre.' Well, Dick, a day or so before Xmas the Youth Centre held another Banquet, to it they invited as guest of honour the Hon. Mrs W.B. Pease, the management committee and a few friends of the Centre. The menu consisted of Sausage and Mash, Brussel Sprouts, Plum Pudding with Custard and coffee. Charles Matthews proposed the Loyal Toast and the Chairman of the members' Committee, Kenneth Hancock, proposed Our Guests, which included as I have already said the Hon. Mrs W.B. Pease, Mrs H.W. Leakey, Chairman of the Management Committee, Mr Parr, Warden of Impington Village College, Mr P.C.N. Tyack, Adult Tutor at Impington, Mr J.H. Garner you all know and Dr Eric Smith. We welcomed as friends two who have been of special assistance to us F.A. Porter and C. Lintott, and regretted that for several reasons Mr M.S. Pease, the Chairman of the Parish Council, Miss Murray, Assistant Tutor of Girton College, and Mr Booth, headmaster of Littleton House School were unable to attend. Mr A.J. Parr responded for the guests and I, as President of the Centre, had the honour to propose the Health of our Absent Friends and pay our respects to the Vacant Chair. After recalling the loss sustained by the management Committee and the Centre through the loss of Miss A. Hibbert-Ware, I was able to tell as far as I knew where and how you were. As we toasted you we thought of you in all parts of the world and wished you God Speed and a quick and safe return. Mrs Pease proposed the Past, the Present and the Future. In her lively and really entertaining speech she made the point that in the future we should form within the village a real and true community spirit which would be invaluable, not only in assisting youth but all our phases of existence. The Banquet was thoroughly enjoyed by all and we were delighted that our two Bevin Boys, Tom Evans and Roland Wilson, who were home on leave for the Xmas holidays were able to join us. Our thanks for this enjoyable evening are particularly due to Mrs Jones, the School Cook, who so kindly came from Cambridge not only during her holiday but while her son, a F/O and Pilot was home on leave. To him the Youth Centre and the N.L. offer our congratulations on his recent award of the Distinguished Service Order.

As is usual at this time of the year the Entertainment Committee gave a party to our children at school residing in the Village. Rations for a party such as this can only be obtained for evacuated children, so before I tell you about the party I would like to pay a tribute to all those

Roland Wilson, Bevin Boy

people who gave up their rationed goods to make cakes and to those good ladies of the Entertainment Committee who worked so hard. About 175 children assembled in the Village Institute; after a good feed they amused themselves with community singing and were then entertained by Mr Greenwood, magician and conjurer. Before leaving for home each child was presented with a savings stamp and a small bag of sweets. You may ask, how did you get the sweets? While I was attending our Executive Committee meeting of the Cambridge and County Affiliation of Youth Clubs, Miss E.A. Round, the Secretary and County Youth Organiser, announced that she had received from the British

Children's Comforts Fund, Australia, a box of sweets and would we suggest how they should be distributed. Needless to say I up and spoke about our party, and the committee graciously gave me as president of the Girton Youth Centre 60 lb of sweets for distribution. This quantity would have enabled me to give each child in Girton $4\frac{1}{2}$ oz. each, but after careful consideration I reduced the amount so that I was eventually able to share the sweets with a greater number of children. I discovered that Coton Village through the generosity of Mrs H.J. Gray also had a children's party, so by giving each child 3 oz., both Girton and Coton children, roughly 320 children went home from their party looking as though they had toothache. I should have liked the people in Australia who so kindly helped in this very practical manner to have heard the three hearty cheers the children gave them – or did they? – it was really deafening; they would have been fully rewarded.

Now for the letters. It was grand to receive so many letters and cards containing your good wishes. Many of you when you so kindly wrote to me said 'Will you please convey my thanks to your committee'. If you were referring to the Entertainment Committee, I have already conveyed your thanks; but if you were referring to a Committee which publishes the N.L. I must point out that the N.L. is written solely by me and all statements with the exception of that which may be written in a postscript are a personal communication from me to you. I am not mentioning this with the desire that I should receive your praise and thanks but to make it quite clear that what is written in the N.L. is an expression of my own personal opinion and in no way an official and studied statement by any committee. It is possible that I may be misinformed from time to time or that the interpretation I may place on the doings and events of various organisations may not be quite what they mean. However, I shall continue to do my utmost to be as factual as possible, but I do hope you will continue to bear the above matter in mind when reading the N.L. The first card came from E.J. Stearn serving with the R.E.s in the Middle East. Congratulations on your well deserved promotion to W.O. The next card bearing good wishes and greetings came from Jack Collings serving on H.M.S. Illustrious somewhere at sea. An Airgraph from Miss Jean Macalister in Palestine tells of her appreciation of the N.L. She says 'I am very happy up here among the orange groves etc., but I am looking forward to seeing Girton again'. Thank you Miss Macalister for your good wishes. Cliff Hankin wrote from the General Hospital, Halifax, where he has been for the past five weeks, to say that he hoped to be discharged from Hospital in the near future and come home on leave. I have not seen him in the village – I do hope that does not signify that he has not recovered. He himself makes the remark that 'It does not pay to look forward to leave you are likely to be disappointed'. I have already mentioned Dick Evans' letter. I have also received one from his twin brother Tom, in which he sends his best wishes for a happy New Year to all his friends at home and abroad. Another old friend Carlos Griffiths in the Far East sent greetings to all his pals. I thank and reciprocate your good wishes to myself. I was so glad to hear that you are well. Another long and interesting letter came from Miss K. Parfitt; she described the jolly time they had on Xmas and Boxing Day; it all sounded very gay and happy. She too sends greetings and best wishes for the coming year. I was glad to hear that you enjoyed yourself so much. Finally a long letter was received from Les Impey. I passed your good wishes on to Miss Wallis and she joins with me in thanking you for your very kind remarks. We both felt that we do not deserve all the kind things you said about us but it did make us feel that the effort of writing the N.L. was worth while.

Tom Evans, Bevin Boy

That's all for this month. So once again as always,
May I wish you God Speed and Good Luck,
Yours very sincerely,
F.C. Barrett.

6 Church Lane,
Girton.
March 1945

Dear

This month the N.L. enters its third year of publication. It hardly seems possible that two years have past since the first N.L. was typed and forwarded to members of the Youth Centre and the Young Men's Group. I have no exact record how many people did receive that first copy, certainly not more than 20, now I deliver roughly a hundred copies to your houses every month to be forwarded to you. Who would have thought when we started the N.L. that it would have to go out to all parts of the world where the sons and daughters of the village are serving. I must admit that writing and delivering the N.L. has involved a great deal of work but it has been one of the joys (and I can assure you, joys have been few and far between during the war) to receive your letters containing your expressions of thanks and appreciation. I feel rather ashamed of my poor efforts after reading about your doings and experiences. The N.L. is written primarily for you who have been away from home for a year or more, for I'm sure after that time you begin to get out of touch with the old village and it is my hope that when you come home you will not feel that there has been a gap in your life.

One of the many things which cannot be conveyed to you is the changing stature of our children, many of them you will not recognise, some who were at school when first you went are now trained soldiers and are serving overseas. I often think about the members of our Youth Centre when first we started our activities, how young they all seemed, now 13 of them are serving their country either in India, Australia, or the European theatre of operations. The physical features are much the same as when you went away. Some of you will miss the church railings but all of you will miss the three large elm trees which stood opposite the church on the little corner site known as the park. These trees were unsafe, there had been several narrow escapes from falling branches, so the Hibbert-Ware Memorial Committee decided after most careful consideration that it would be best to uproot them before they proceeded with their plans for laying out the garden. It always grieves me to see a beautiful tree come crashing down, but as these trees were neither beautiful nor safe it was probably the best to cut them down;

nevertheless, it does seem to have created a yawning gap now they are no more. We shall get used to it in a short time and when the garden is planted we shall feel it was ever thus. Building has been suspended, we haven't even had a couple of farm worker's cottages erected in the village. The houses already in existence are all beginning to look shabby and unkempt for they all seem to require a coat of paint and those little attentions so necessary to keep a house in repair. I hope this state of affairs will not continue long for I fully agree with Mr Pease who in a recent N.L. said 'Housing is the most important item after winning the war'. Housing is really acute; rooms, or accommodation in a parent's house may be all right for a short time but there is no pleasure in trying to bring up a family in two rooms, or where there may be restrictions and inconveniences. A Housing Committee was elected as part of the Reconstruction Committee at the last Annual Parish Meeting; their mandate was, I believe, to survey and advise the Parish Council in Housing requirements in the village. I haven't heard how this committee is progressing or what are its proposals – I'll have to get my spies to work and try and find out for you.

We have had our share of the severe weather that seemed to be general in this country and on the continent. The sharp frosts made the ground so hard that the farm workers were unable to work on the land and we bemoaned the fact that due to such efficient methods of land drainage there was no ice near the village on which we could skate. The lads of the village had to cycle to the Sewage Farm at Milton or go to the Willows at Chesterton where they had to pay a 1/– if they wished to besport themselves on the ice.

The Homecoming Fund Committee have got down to work and I am informed by Mr W. Dixon that they are already nearing the first £200. He also told me that at a recent Whist Drive they almost topped the £20 mark, and that plans have been prepared for a series of Concerts, Variety Shows, Dances, etc., to be held during this month. Next month it is proposed to have a grand Homecoming Week, commencing on Easter Sunday with a concert, on Monday a Whist Drive and Dance, on Tuesday the Youth Centre are going to hold a grand Fun Fair in the Village Institute, on Wednesday Mr Whitehead presents a Film Show, on Thursday Marshall's Concert party, and on Friday Dr Walton's Wardens are getting up to some tricks, details at the time of writing are not known. The item for Saturday has not yet been arranged, but I'm sure on Sunday those of us who are still left with our boots might be seen visiting 'Uncles' where we will be trying to raise the wind for our next week's rations! Still, all good wishes to those enterprising people – may they have a record week!

The Village Education Society had a joint meeting with the Youth Centre and they listened to a most interesting lecture given by Miss E.A. Round, the County Youth Organiser, on 'The Service of Youth'. Miss Round surveyed the work of the voluntary bodies such as Church organisations, Scouts, Guides, etc., and showed that they did a fine job of work extremely well but unfortunately they only touched the fringe of the problem. When the war came juvenile delinquency rapidly increased, so the Government produced its now famous Circular 1486 which promised grant aid for local Youth work from the Board of Education. This grant is payable to voluntary bodies as well as those approved by the local Authority. Miss Round concluded her talk with an account of the work already done in our county for which the Local Authority is responsible, and summarised the aims of this work, which, briefly, are as follows: We must care for individuals and widen their interests, help them to think clearly and quickly, to have healthy and physically fit bodies and above all help them to develop a standard of behaviour and philosophy in their lives and in their dealings with their fellows, so that from the Youth Centre we may expect to develop a democratic community with citizenship in its widest sense.

The Allotment Society has already distributed early seed potatoes to its members in preparation for planting, and one day this week the Society held a 'Brains Trust' in the Village Institute on gardening matters.

The rough weather has stopped most football matches including those of our village team; they managed to defeat Impington 4–3 in their last match.

It was grand to meet Lt. Jack Wakelin home on leave from Belgium; he is as far as I know the first Girton man to come home on leave from the B.A.D.

Letters have been received from far and near; space does not allow them to be published in detail but I wish to thank you very much indeed. I realise under what difficulties you have to write and that makes them doubly appreciated. And now to the letters. I must first acknowledge a letter received from an old friend 'Midge' Ellis which I received about Xmas time and then mislaid. Midge sends greetings to all members of the Youth Centre and his friends in the Forces.

Two grand letters have been received from 'Gummy' Naylor; he tells me that he has been to New York, Panama, Society Islands, New Hebrides and New Guinea. He like Midge sends greetings to the Youth Centre and all his pals.

The India Command was represented by an airgraph from J. Hind and letters from B. Kidman and Ronny Lipscombe. They all express their appreciation of the N.L. and say they read it several times over, even though it is a few months old when they get it. Claude discussed the Reconstruction Committee's proposals and hopes that they will have plenty of support. 'Ronny' says he is in touch with Jack Collings, Arthur Evans, C. Kidman and L. Hales, but so far he hasn't met them. All send best wishes to readers of the N.L. at home and abroad.

Corporal J Hind, R.A.F.

Les Impey in Italy wrote an interesting letter, how I wished I could quote all of it. He had many points about the Community Centre which will be helpful.

Finally, letters were received from two old friends, Miss K. Parfitt and John Chapman. Miss Parfitt thinks the 'Welcome Home Fund' is a grand idea, and makes suggestions for the distribution of the Homecoming Fund. I will pass on your suggestions to the authorities concerned. John sends greetings and good wishes to you all.

The postscript is written by P/O Frank Dupont, well known to the members of the Young Men's Group, and is associated with the activities of the Baptist Chapel. We welcome his contribution as from a Service man – what about a P.S. from a Service woman?

That is all for this month, so once again as always, may I wish you good luck and God speed.
Yours very sincerely,
F.C. Barrett.

POSTSCRIPT

For me a Service man's dream has come true! At the moment I am actually billeted at home! Although one only sees the village in the early morning and late evening, some opportunity has been given to see Girton in war time.

Many of the reminders of the war have already shed their garb and the village in most respects appears its normal self. The missing faces are the most noticeable alteration. The First-Aid Party has long since ceased to man Mr Searle's hut and the Recreation Ground to house the Searchlight and other defences. The recent standing-down of the Home Guard closes a chapter of hard unselfish service difficult to equal, and the village is justly proud of the men who trained so wholeheartedly in order that, should the need arise, our homes and loved ones would be well and truly protected. The police, Wardens and Fire Services are still on the alert and the people at home have been enabled to sleep in peace, knowing that their friends too were well trained and always ready. Other blokes and the ladies also – God Bless 'em – have done their part in so many ways, in factories and shops, on the land, on the buses and in helping to provide our families with food and clothing and perhaps most important of all in keeping our homes together and looking after the little ones. There are others too, who have served right well that space forbids mention of here.

Yes chums, we can well feel proud of the folks we left behind us and can rely on them to keep on doing their stuff until Victory is ours and one by one we get back into civvies and take our part in village life once more.

We are grateful also to folk who have continued to care for the interests of the children and young people, for those who have worked so hard on the Entertainment Committee, in order to swell the Forces Fund, and last but by no means least, to our very good friend Mr Barrett, for compiling and sending us this News Letter. Do we realise that this N.L. is a One Man Show and consider the very considerable amount of work entailed? It's a rattling good show and to Mr Barrett and Miss Wallis, who does the typing, we say 'Thank you very much indeed'.

When peace follows victory what a team there will be in Girton! Those who have kept everything going so well at home plus the warriors returned from all parts of the world. Yes, what a team, provided all are playing on the same side. One of the few good things that come out of war is the uniting of peoples in a common effort and I do believe that our village is more united than ever before. There must be different styles of play but that is all to the good and helps to make the game both interesting and successful. The main point to remember is that all must be striving in their different ways to achieve the same end, shall we say to score through the same goal! What then is the goal for post-war Girton? To produce a community of Happy, Healthy and Useful Citizens – young, middle life, and old, Church and Chapel or neither, rich, middle class or poor. Let us play hard, work hard and if necessary fight hard against anything that would stand between ourselves and that goal. Every organisation in the village is doing something in the village to help achieve this object, here's wishing them all more strength to their elbows! Let all who have remained and all who will return, be tolerant, of good will and active and the future of Girton will be bright indeed.

The Baptist Chapel, spiritual home of Frank Dupont

It was my privilege recently to attend a Concert given by the extremely able 'Girton Juvenile Follies'. To watch and listen to those youngsters made one realise that it was worth going through hell now and refraining from taking things too easily when the job is finished. We must ensure a happy future for them.

In the words of Tiny Tim, God Bless us Every One.

Frank Dupont

6 Church Lane,
Girton.
April 1945

Dear

For the past few weeks I have been wondering what on earth I could write about this month. I have scratched my head time and time again, and hoped that some great event would occur in the village so that I could elaborate upon it. Usually I find someone to write a postscript for me, but I am sorry to say that this month I have been quite unable to get anyone to write one. Now talking of postscripts, what about one of you having a go? I receive quite a number of interesting letters from you from time to time, but usually they are mixed up with personal matters, therefore somewhat unsuitable for publication. What about writing an open letter to your pals in other theatres of operations? I will, if you so desire publish it, and then hope it will induce others to reply. We could hear how you are prospering, what the country in which you are serving is like and all the new ideas you have developed and how those ideas could be incorporated into our village life. I say quite frankly, we here at home, are looking forward to your return in order that our village community may be strengthened and broadened with your views and ideas.

This letter is dated April, but as I have told you on previous occasions I am writing it a month in advance. The poet said 'Oh, to be in England now that April's there', you will probably echo these same sentiments. Can I recall to you what it all looks like? The snowdrops, and crocuses in the grounds of Girton College, how beautiful they have been, the winter rain and the glorious sunshine of the past few weeks have contributed to make a really fine display. The hedgerows are bursting into leaf and in the early morning the bird's song fills the air. On the allotments everyone, including myself, are to be seen in the hour or so between leaving off work and the falling of dusk, working away to get the digging completed. I must admit that I have worked all day on Sundays to do this job, and I now feel somewhat aggrieved that after all my labour Mr Jack North has purchased a Trusty Tractor with which he is willing to plough and harrow one's allotment for a reasonable sum. When I think of all the toil

Girton College, where students also helped to 'Dig for Victory'

and sweat I put into digging my allotment and all this could have been avoided had I known that Mr North anticipated purchasing such a useful machine!!

Our football team has had to withdraw from the Youth Sports Football League. This has been caused by the difficulty of raising a side; earlier in the season this was possible as we had more lads, but what with the 'call-up', and the fact that some of the lads have Thursday afternoon off one week and Saturday afternoon another, it became an anxiety to raise a team. Several away fixtures had to be cancelled through this cause and as we could see no possibility of fitting in the fixtures at a later date there was no alternative but to withdraw from the league, much to the disappointment of everyone, as Girton held fifth place in the league table.

The Girton Choral Society, of which Mr L.N. Tingey is the instructor and conductor, gave another delightful concert on a recent Sunday evening. Never have I seen the Village Institute so tastefully decorated – probably some of you have not been inside the hall since the stage was built; the curtains and wings are very dismal as the only material available at the time of building was blackout cloth – those curtains were withdrawn and in their place were festoons of ivy interlaced with crocuses. At the back of the stage Mrs Burgess had exquisitely painted a rural scene with its castle, fields, flowers and streams which gave background when those delightful songs of Cambridgeshire, which were composed by Mr Tingey were sung by the Choir. This concert was given in order to raise funds to enable the choir to compete in the Musical Festival at Impington Village College.

Another enterprising Society in the Village is the Education Society, they are inviting Mr Henry Morris, the Chief Education Officer for the County to give a talk about Education and the Community Centre. This should be an important lecture for us in view of the interest already aroused by the Reconstruction Committee's recommendations in this subject. I hope to attend this and the Annual Parish meeting which is to be held on the 28th March, and will give you details of these meetings next month.

The Homecoming Fund is going from strength to strength, at a recent whist drive and dance the takings for the evening amounted to £45, which I'm sure you will agree was a fine effort. The Youth Centre continues its activities, their popular dances are still going strong; a few evenings ago Dr Cam, lecturer in History at Girton College, brought three students to the Centre and held a Model Parliamentary Election. Each of the three students spoke for approximately ten minutes, during this time they attempted to place the views and policy of the Liberal, Labour and Conservative parties before the members. After the speeches the Candidates were questioned as to their parties policy on such questions as Poland, Education, how to avoid unemployment when Service men and women return home, Nationalisation of land, mines and railways. The result of the voting was that the Liberal was returned by one vote over the Labour opponent; the Conservative only polling two votes.

Talking about the Youth Centre, I was pleased to meet Bryan Betts, our 'Baby' in the forces, home on leave. He has been transferred from the Infantry to the Royal Corps of Signals. He brought news of another old member David Martlew. David is working in the Research Department of the Rolls Royce Factory somewhere in the Midlands, I understand that he is assisting with high altitude flying, according to Bryan he does a lot of flying and has at the same time managed to pass his inter-B.Sc. examination. Congratulations David.

At long last Cliff Hankin has come home on leave after five months in Hospital. He looks well but he told me that he has to return to convalescent home for a month or so before he can rejoin his unit. He expected to get home for Xmas, how true his words were when he said 'you can never rely on leave when you're in the Army'.

I was surprised and pleased to meet, the other day, another old friend, Dick Diver of Histon. He has been discharged from the Army because of an old injury which he received while playing football some years ago. He had hoped that by now the injury would have recovered, but long route marches aggravated it and it became impossible to continue. From him I heard that Eric (Hocker) Smith was temporarily having a rough time due to some form of stomach trouble, apart from that Eric had been enjoying army life and had been playing in some good class football. I was sorry to hear that another village lad, Harry Chapman is an invalid. Harry by some means, still unknown to us, has broken his arm; he is convalescing in Southern Italy, and by his cheery letters he is well on the way to recovery.

Harry J Chapman, R.A.S.C.

Mr Charles Gawthrop showed me the other day a recent photograph of his son Sid. Italy must be really suiting Sid for he looked as though he has put on a bit of weight. His Dad told me that when he was in Italy during the last war the climate suited him and he too put on weight, but after a spell in a German prison camp he returned to the familiar figure we all know so well today.

George Betson, R.A.S.C.

It was a pleasure to meet Harry Cranfield and George Betson home on leave from the B.L.A. Harry surprised me when he told me that he had been in the army $5\frac{1}{2}$ years. I readily remembered that he was in the Norwegian Campaign, which was fought in the early days of the war. I asked him what he would like to do when he returned to 'Civvy Street', Harry's laconic reply was 'I hardly dare to think about that day, you never know, I might yet be sent to Burma to fight the Japs!' Tony, Harry's brother is serving on H.M.S. Howe, I think I am right in saying it is Admiral Bruce Frazer's Flagship, the ship has figured in the news quite a lot lately for its aggressive attacks on Jap islands.

Talking of islands, reminds me that Robert Burrows has returned from the Azores, that group of islands in mid-Atlantic after being stationed there for the past year. I haven't seen him but his Mother tells me he is very fit. His brother John has recently, through the ballot, become a 'Bevin Boy'.

Many of you will be sorry to hear of the death of Mrs Kate Scott, the wife of Mr A. Scott, who was for many years licensee of the Old Crown. The N.L. also regrets to record the death of Pte. E. Pigden of the Royal Army Catering Corps, who was killed on active service on Feb. 13th. Pte Pigden evacuated his wife and children from London at the outbreak of hostilities. Before joining the army he worked on a number of aerodromes in the district as a bricklayer. To his wife and five children, all of school age, we extend our sincere sympathy.

And now for the letters: the first came from Tom Impey in which he said, 'You have probably heard that I am in the Jungle in Burma and another one of Girton's lads to join the 14th Army'. On the whole Tom fares well for food although at times it gets monotonous being generally tinned or dehydrated. However he says 'that with an occasional piece of fresh fish, which I am getting expert at catching, I manage quite well. I guess the hook and bit of dough is a novelty to them, and we are naturally reaping a harvest while we can'. Tom continues, 'I read with great interest your news of the Welcome Home Fund, I think it is a great idea and I eagerly look forward to the time when all the lads and lasses meet again'. With reference to the Homecoming Fund, Tom makes the remarks 'None of us can decide for ourselves where and how we shall serve, home or overseas, therefore all should be treated the same'. Tom has met Claude Kidman and is continually on the look-out for a familiar face. To his brother in Italy and all his friends at home and abroad, he sends greetings and best wishes and hopes that he may soon have that long awaited pint at home.

An Airgraph from 'Gummy' Naylor somewhere in the Pacific concludes 'Our one big hope now is that the month is not far off when you will write your Grand Final N.L. which will be at the end of the war. I think if circumstances permit we shall have to have that a decorated affair which can be kept as a souvenir'. Well, Gummy I'll see what I can do, and as soon as possible. Another letter from S.E.A.C. came from Len Hales; after expressing his appreciation of the N.L. he says 'I have an idea that Arthur Evans is in this area, I'm hoping to have the pleasure of meeting him. Tell him through the N.L. that if he should at any time come across any Tank Transporter Vehicles to ask if they are '553 Coy', should it happen that they are, all the lads know me very well and would forward any message, by doing so I think there is a good chance of meeting (but I hope he doesn't bring his mules they don't seem very friendly), that goes for any other local lads; incidentally it's the Assam Burma Front'. He says that although he has served 5 years 3 mths; 3 years abroad; he feels that there should be an equal distribution of the Homecoming Fund to all who have served. Finally, he sends greetings and best wishes to all at home and abroad, and especially to Les Impey.

My ever faithful correspondent, John Chapman, sent his usual letter for which I am most grateful. John, I should like to meet you when you are home on leave next time.

To you all, thank you for your letters, and may I again send you my best wishes. To you as always, Good luck and God speed. Yours very sincerely,
F.C. Barrett.

6 Church Lane,
Girton.
May 1945

Dear

Last month when I wrote to you I said that I had hoped that some great event would occur in the village so that I could elaborate upon it and fill the N.L. No great event has happened in the village but indeed great events are happening in the European theatres of operations. It seems incredible that since I wrote the last N.L. the Rhine has been crossed and our armies have advanced too, at the time of writing, the outskirts of Berlin. People here at home are asking 'How Long' and the usual reply is 'Any day now'. We all realise that it has not been such an easy walk over as the popular press has made out, we have watched and waited with almost bated breath, as the strong points of Holland and the Northern Ports are liberated and we have wondered if the British lads will have the opportunity of marching into Berlin with the Russians and the Americans. Many people with whom I have spoken have expressed the view that the British lads have participated in the hardest fighting along the road to Berlin via Caen, Holland and Hamburg. Theirs has not been an easy task but we are glad to say that so far no village lad has fallen a casualty during the recent offensive.

I believe that I have interpreted the mood of the people here at home when I say there would be little or no enthusiasm for a V. Day if it were to be proclaimed immediately Berlin falls. There are many tough spots which require clearing up, Italy, the Channel ports, Norway and Denmark. There would be a feeling of unreality if we celebrated Victory and had still this work to do. Speaking more particularly of our own village I'm sure there will be little or no enthusiasm for V Day while we still have to face the Japs. Although we read in our newspapers more about the work of the European armies, our village, in common with many of our East Anglian neighbours take an equal interest in the 'Forgotten Army'. I would not for a moment let you fellows out in Burma or India think you are forgotten men, you are not, and your victory over the Japs at Mandalay was acclaimed by all as a very fine job of work. You are not forgotten in the matter of reinforcements either, I seem to recall that in an earlier N.L. I said Girton men were on the way to the front so the 'Jerries' would have to look out; knocked out would have been a much better expression. Now our village lads are on their way to India. Tom Palmer, Reg Cundell and Reg Holt have recently arrived, and combined with you folks on the spot will present us with a real V. Day which we can all without reservation join in.

As a result of the now changed position in the west we are to have all blackout and dimout regulations removed, it is these little things – or are they the big things? – which make life more easy. If we could only have a few more household goods such as cooking pots, towels and clothes, life would become easier – however, we are grateful and thankful for all our present blessings and these other things will be added unto us in due course.

I attended the meeting of the Village Education Society at which Mr Morris, Chief Education Officer for the County spoke about education and the Community Centre. He had little to add to his previous talk which he gave earlier in the year to the Reconstruction Committee, he did make however what I considered to be a valuable suggestion 'That the people of Girton should make plans, not drawings, and surveys of all the requirements for the proposed Community Centre. These should include all aspects such as Assembly Hall, Junior School, Library, Changing rooms and showers, so that if any one part of the plan received immediate approval it could be proceeded with and at the same time the whole would be in mind and we could plan not only a convenient and useful building but also one of a pleasing design.' A further point was, I think implied rather than said, that as there are few Community Centres in existence it would be a good thing for the village as far as financial assistance was concerned, if Girton was first in the field, they might more readily get grants from the Philanthropic bodies.

Girton Glebe School, opened in 1951

It was interesting to read C.E.M.A.'s fifth annual report which was published last week, in it was stated 'That as soon as labour and material are free there must be a real drive for Community

Centres' – premises that are devoted to the general leisure and pleasure as well as to the graces of life. As you may have gathered I am very keen about the idea of a Community Centre, it will be available for all, and it will be a means whereby we might better enjoy, as I have just said, the leisure and pleasures of life. Surely these are the very things for which you and your comrades fought; we can and will look forward to 'Welcome home' All who have served, but what of our debt to those who are not returning to those we knew so well and who have lost their lives? You I'm sure would be the first to agree that our indebtedness cannot be met by our appreciation only of survivors. I personally, may I here stress the word personally, feel that our gratitude must be made manifest by some permanent memorial – a memorial not only 'In grateful memory' but in service of those for whose sakes the fallen made their sacrifice. It was, surely for the right to the pursuit of happiness and knowledge that our friends gave their lives, and I feel that we should do all in our power to provide those who follow after the opportunity which the fallen so desired. It is with these thoughts in mind that I suggest that our Entertainment and Homecoming Committees might after they have completed their allotted tasks combine and provide a nucleus for a form of a Community Centre.

The Annual Parish Meeting was held on March 25th, in the Village Institute. I always look forward each year to this meeting, it is so democratic, at it you can hear about the activities of the village, you can criticise, applaud or just sit, there is an opportunity to suggest to you 'Village Fathers' new ideas for the betterment of the village. I have a further interest in the meeting, it provides me with 'copy' for the N.L. and gives me possible clues as to which way the 'wind may blow' in the future. This year, two days before the meeting I was smitten with the Flu, but in spite of that I made up my mind to attend the meeting. I swallowed aspirins, drank proprietary medicines that are supposed to 'cure you while you wait', but a few minutes before the meeting I had to admit defeat and retire to bed and stay there until I was able to convalesce a week later. However, I have since questioned many people about the proceedings, Mr Pease very kindly sent me an agenda paper, and combined with the report in the local press, I will be able to give you a resume of the proceedings. Mr Pease presided and about 60 residents attended. Mr Pease gave a report on the work of the Council during the past year and he called attention to the difficulty of keeping in good order the recreation ground and the village green and expressed the hope that the residents would see their property did not suffer wilful damage. As one of the School managers, he reported that whilst great difficulty had arisen in the Girton School from shortage of staff and illness during the passed winter the results were satisfactory. He also made the suggestion that it might be possible next term to open a nursery class at the village school; I have since learnt that Miss A Garner, daughter of the present Headmaster has recently been appointed to the school staff and will be by virtue of her special training, qualified to open the above nursery class. A report from the Reconstruction Committee referred to recent circular on Community Centres and also to the details with which you should now be familiar through reading the N.L.

You will recall that I said that I would get my spies to work to find out what the sub-committee on housing had been doing, well it was reported that no meeting had been called owing to the fact that no indication of the Government's intentions had been received. It was agreed that a resolution deploring the lack of any well defined Government policy be sent to the R.D.C. asking them to press this matter with the Ministry concerned. The accounts of the Town Charity, Village Institute, Salvage and the Entertainment Committee were presented and passed. The Village Education Society gave their report and the Secretary of the Homecoming Fund, Mr Dixon reported on the success of this venture. They have already passed the £200 mark. Mrs Leakey referring to the balance sheet of the Alice Hibbert-Ware Memorial Fund said that the total amount subscribed, £552, showed the great respect in which this lady was held. It was hoped that the site for the memorial garden would soon be cleared and planted. Finally, Mr Pease reported that owing to failing health Mr Skinner had resigned as representative of the R.D.C. and it was agreed to send Mr Skinner a letter of thanks and appreciation for all the work he had done on behalf of the village.

It was grand to meet T. Cox home on leave after serving 3 years in Ceylon, his praise for the N.L. made me feel somewhat embarrassed, but I did appreciate his kind remarks. Maurice Songer has also arrived home from the Middle East, I have not had the pleasure of meeting him but his Mother told me that he is very fit.

The N.L. sends hearty congratulations to Jack Wakelin on his promotion to the rank of Captain. The grand Homecoming Week was a great success. A draw was organised by the Committee, and raised a total of £104. A dance, held on Easter Monday attracted a large crowd, and I think a total of £45 was raised at this function. On Tuesday the Youth Centre ran a Funfair, a place where money seemed so easy to make, but on returning home you found that you were 'stony'. The evening was most enjoyable, and I think people had their money's worth; anyway it was good to be able to present the Fund with a cheque for £13.10s. On Wednesday Mr Whitehead organised a film show, and on Thursday the Wardens took over and held a social evening for the young people. Friday a grand Whist drive, and on Saturday the Girton Follies gave their now famous show. Altogether the week brought in a grand total of £167 by this fine effort, and I really think all who organised it are to be congratulated.

And now for the letters. The first came from L/Cpl. Rue Scott serving with the C.M.F. After thanking us for the N.L. he says 'although I have been away from the old village for several years, I am always ready for news of what is going on.' He continues 'I'm afraid most of the lads you mention in your letters are strangers to me, but I was interested to read in one letter that Stan Hankin and Sid Gawthrop are in this country (Italy) and had met, maybe I shall run across them one of these days, also my cousin Harry Chapman.' He wishes to be remembered to Mr Ray and Vic Watson, Reg Gawthrop and Mr J.H. Garner. Jack Collings who is serving on H.M.S. Illustrious sends greetings and best wishes to all at home and abroad, he says that he is looking forward to coming home although he recently spent a 48hrs leave with some people and they fed him on a marvellous variety of food, fruit, milk shakes and ice cream; and then he adds, quite unnecessarily, I did full justice to everything!

Another sailor from the village, Tony Cranfield sent me a long and interesting letter, he tells me that his ship is serving with the Americans and that he just missed seeing his cousin Dick, I believe his ship sailed into harbour as Dick's sailed out. Tony concludes by saying how much he looks forward to playing football when he returns home and hopes that day won't be long.

The final letter came from Carlos Griffiths, serving in a British Hospital in Burma. He enjoys the N.L. very much, and at the time of writing was in the best of health. He says I look out to see if any of the village lads might come in, as much as I would like to see them I would not care for them to become casualties or sick. He is in contact by letter with A. Evans, and was in the forward area with the troops which captured Kohima. Carlos continues 'The corner of the park will look bare with those elms down. I can remember when I was at school, Dick Evans fell down one of those and broke his arm.' Yes, Carlos, I was there that afternoon when Dick broke his arm. I had recently purchased the piece of land on which my house now stands, and I was trying to get the garden round when I saw some of the school children swinging on the ends of the branches of the trees, not very high up, about 3 or 4' from the ground; I now know Dick slipped and in trying to save himself broke his arm. Someone fetched Mr Garner, who splinted the fracture and I can still vividly recall thinking what a fine job he made of it. I went and 'phoned' for the ambulance and someone else fetched Dick's father. Let Mr Garner now take up the story – he recalled the incident but the thing that interested him most was when Mr Evans appeared he had to push back Dick's hair in order to find a scar which was his only means of identifying Dick from Tom. His only remark when he discovered the culprit was 'Oh! I thought it would be you, what have you been up to now'. Mr Garner told me that during the time those two lads were at school he could not tell 't'other from which' and always had to ask the other children which was Tom and which was Dick. I can tell the difference now, but I never worried after I discovered that his Father required definite proof before he could decide which was which. Carlos concludes his letter with the request that I send him the address of C. Kidman and R. Lipscombe. I will do that but I am publishing your address so that they or any other Girtonian can get in touch with you. Carlos' address is as follows – 7406030 Pte. C.J. Griffiths, B.M.H., Shillong, S.E.A.C.

Well that is all for this month, thank you for your letters, and may I again send you my best wishes. To you all as always, Good luck and God speed.
Yours very sincerely,
F.C. Barrett.

6 Church Lane,
Girton.
June 1945

Dear

I must apologise for last month's N.L. It must have seemed out of date when you got it for even before I delivered it to your homes the war in Europe was over and V.E. Day had been celebrated. Still I know you understand. You who are abroad must have been at home in thought on V.E. Day. What was it like in Girton? Did the people rejoice? Were the flags out? Did the George and the Crown have a full house? These and many more questions you must have asked several times over.

As you know, the news of the final overthrow of Nazi Germany was expected as the Germans had themselves announced by radio their unconditional surrender; while this was unofficial it did give many people a chance to prepare for the promised two days' holiday – or as we had anticipated part of V.E. Day and the day following. It also gave some of my colleagues an opportunity to prepare a fine cocktail, for it was almost certain we would not have to come to work on the following day. When we left our employment we toasted 'Peace and Happiness, long may they reign'. As I rode home I passed through a growing and mixed variety of flags until I came to Girton, where many smiling faces were eagerly discussing the immediate possibility of peace.

After tea I joined my comrades of the Entertainment Social Committee with the purpose of discussing with the Homecoming Social Committee, plans for a proposed Grand Garden Fete to be held in the recreation ground on August Bank Holiday. Instead of discussing this we turned our attention to what could be arranged for V.E. night. It was decided to hold a social free of charge for all the village children in the Village Institute and a dance for their parents in the 'Women's Institute', also free of charge. While we were discussing the details, a message from the Committee of the W.I. stated that they had much pleasure in loaning their hall free of charge, this was quickly followed by one from the Youth Centre offering their radio-gram also free of charge. All arrangements now made, we left the meeting in time to hear the 9 o'clock news and as we passed the Rec gate the Youth Centre boys were to be seen building a large pile of wood, straw and any burnable material they could lay their hands on in preparation for a bonfire. The finished pile was about as high as the Pavilion and it was surmounted by an effigy of Hitler holding a swastika flag – however more about this in a moment.

V.E. day dawned and people were out early hanging out flags of all shapes and sizes, some bought especially for this day, some saved from the Coronation, and I'm sure many people improvised, like we did and cut up coloured materials to make bunting – though I must say I was taken aback when I realised that it was some of my old football jerseys in the form of bunting which was blowing in the breeze. I do not know anything about signalling by means of flags, but I was told that one house in the village was flying 'Fever aboard' and 'Drop the Pilot', however it all went to make the village look and feel gay.

At mid-day a united service of thanksgiving was held in the Church, and as the people were assembling the air was filled with the roar of fully laden Lancaster bombers on their way to Holland to feed the starving population. Truly were our hearts filled with thankfulness that the war in Europe was over and that again we could turn our attention to the living instead of the destruction of life.

An Avro Lancaster, symbol to many of British air power

In the evening we held the children's social which was attended by a large number who fully enjoyed themselves with games, dancing and community singing, and at the end, with the glasses of lemonade, which were kindly provided by Mrs Turner to relieve their parched throats. When the function was over it was getting dusk and on the Rec the Y.C. lads were waiting with approximately 10 gallons of what would have filled 'Molotov Cocktails' had the Germans invaded, ready for the word 'Go'. When it was considered dark enough, one of them climbed to the top of the pile, and soaked Hitler to the skin and generally saturated everything. A lighted match was thrown and with a roar the flames rose to the height of the Church, fireworks were lit, and Mrs Pease, her days of umpiring incidents over, was seen lighting 'thunderflashes', whilst in another corner Capt. R. Gane of the Home Guard, fully experienced in handling pyrotechnics, was also creating loud bangs! The flames rose higher, giving an eerie light to the trees and to the Church building; all the people present joined hands and danced round the fire, and I thought then what a happy time it was, and what thoughts and memories must be in everyone's mind – thankful that six years of misery are now behind us.

With the fire still burning we wended our way down to the W.I., where the hall was packed to capacity, everyone enjoying themselves. I doubt if the village has spent such a happy, but in spirit an essentially quiet day, for a long time; all the fun was of a spontaneous nature marked by dignity and restraint, and many minds were fixed on the distant war which has yet to be won. On the following evening the W.I. organised another dance, and they kindly divided the proceeds £13.10s. between the Homecoming and Entertainment Committees, the £10 collected on the previous evening was similarly divided. And now what else has been happening in the village? During the first days of May we were subjected to severe frosts and days of snow and sleet. As the fruit blossom was forward, due to the early warm weather a fair amount of damage was sustained by the fruit growers. I do not think it is quite as bad as anticipated for the fruit was sufficiently developed to withstand the frost. During the week 6–12th May, the Cambridge Borough and County Youth Clubs, and Youth Organisations held what was termed a Festival of Youth. The idea behind it all was to demonstrate to the public what our young people could do if given the opportunity. There were many displays of P.T., handicrafts, drama and such like activities. We, here in Girton, were invited to share in the Festival, but as our facilities are few, we were unable to take part in any of the foregoing displays. We did however, do something which was original and worthwhile and that was an Exhibition of Girton, Past, Present, and our hopes for the Future. We searched the village for exhibits, and almost every house was prevailed upon to find photographs of the early Village, articles of interest etc. We managed to get for the Past section, photographs and records of the Anglo-Saxon and Roman relics which were found when Girton College was built, some old agricultural implements, some were found in Mr Searle's workshop, old maps on which the name of Girton was spelt Gyton, Gritton, Gaton, Gatoon, etc., a 19th Century dinner, old dresses and clothing and some most interesting photographs of Girton College. Did you know that Girton College was built in an open field and that the trees were planted after the building had been erected? A section was devoted to the Church Building and this included rubbings from the brasses in the chancel, a survey of the tombstones in the burial ground and some interesting records taken from the Parish register, and some fine views and drawings of the building. Much fun and comments were centred around the display of photographs of the village, and village personalities of days gone by, which included many school groups of children who are now grand- or great-grand parents! Sporting pictures were there in plenty, old football and cricket teams. The famous Girton Cycling Club of 1916 called the Slow Wheelers. Do any of you recall it? Mr Budden in a grand blazer, Mr White and Mr Thulbourne and quite a number who are no longer with us. What I should have liked, and I patiently searched the village without success, was a photograph of the old drum and fife band. I believe Mr Jack North was bandmaster, Mr Bert Cole and Mr G. Hawkes and a few more were members. Mr Cole told me they were very good and used to go round the village playing. They were allowed to practice in the coach house attached to what is now Mrs Leakey's house. Mrs Anna Maria Cotton bought the instruments for them, and they paid her back at 6d a week. One day goes the tale, they were playing in the village and stopped outside the George and the Dragon, now the George, and they were invited in to play, which they did, but mark you, they did not have a drink!! Unfortunately the news that they were in the house of refreshment preceded them home. On arrival at their coach house the good lady would have nothing more to do with them and turned them out, and to this day the member of the band who told me of this incident said with great feeling in his voice 'And to think we never had a drink!' I have heard many such amusing stories, but to return to the exhibition. There was a fine display of fauna and flora of the village, this exhibit was prepared by G. Dixon and P. Thomson without any supervision. Finally in the Hopes for the Future section, the future housewife saw a display of Kitchen appliances, and the possibilities which may be hers with dehydrated food. The exhibition was opened by Mr Pease and it remained open for three evenings, Saturday, Monday and Tuesday. In addition to opening the exhibition Mr Pease gave an account of the Enclosure Act and how it affected the life of the village of Girton. He also produced the Enclosure Map and Award. On Monday the Rector (Rev L.G. Tucker) gave an interesting Historical account of the Church building, and in addition to illustrating his talk with photographs, drawings and exhibits, he also produced the earliest parish register still in possession of the Church dated 1623. On the final evening Mr W.P. Baker gave a delightful lantern lecture on Cottages Old and New. This wound up a good piece of work, I wished I had time and space to tell you of all the interesting things I have seen and heard during the past three weeks. However, we may be able to do so some other time.

Now for news in brief: It is with regret that we have to record the death of Mr Frank Skinner and Mr Walliker. Mr Skinner was well known locally and was one of the village representatives on the R.D.C. Mr Walliker had been ill for some time but had recently started working. He collapsed and died very suddenly. To their relatives the N.L. extends its sincere sympathy. With the death of Mr Skinner a vacancy occurs on the Parish Council and the R.D.C. and an election for a representative from the village for the R.D.C. was held in the Men's Institute on the 16th May. Mr Booth, Headmaster of Littleton House School was elected over his opponent Mr Monkman, by a majority of 42 votes. It was I believe a record attendance of electors, which all goes to show how alive our village is.

There are now two vacancies on the Parish Council, the other has been caused by the resignation of Mr Tingey, who is leaving the village. With him go the good wishes and thanks of all the village for organising, in the early days of the War, the First-Aid party. He has also been conductor and tutor of the singing class.

It was grand to meet an old pal, George Pauley, home on leave from Belgium. He looked fit and well, and hopes soon to be home for good. Another old pal came walking down the street a few days before V.E. Day and that was Ronny Lipscombe who has been $2\frac{1}{2}$ years in Ceylon. He too looked exceptionally fit and well and weren't we glad to see him!

And now for the letters – the first came from Arthur Evans. Arthur, I thank you for your very kind remarks. I am so glad to hear that you are well and that you have come through the severe fighting unscathed, in which your battalion has been engaged. We heard a special tribute to the Northants for that piece of work, on the B.B.C. the other day. To all his friends at home and abroad Arthur sends kind regards and good wishes. An Airmail letter from J. Chapman tells me that he is on his way to India. Another Girtonian to swell the soon to be victorious band. A long letter from Harry Chapman in Italy tells me that his arm has now recovered and that he feels fit enough to go back to his unit. He had a good time on V.E. day and wondered how we spent it in Girton. He too, hopes to be home soon but in the meantime sends greetings and best wishes to all.

Walter Purkis, soon to leave the Bahamas, also sends greetings to his Girton friends in the services. He says that he has always looked forward to and thoroughly enjoyed receiving and reading the N.L. and hopes to call upon me in the very near future.

The final letter comes from 'Gummy' Naylor in which he says that it is grand to hear from the N.L. how everyone is, and that it means a great deal to me. It forms a link with home and tells of friends far and wide of which I might never hear until the war is over. He recalls old memories of the searchlight unit on the Rec, the football and cricket teams now disbanded and scattered over the world, which included many who attended your first Y.C. meeting. He also mentions the Park where Dick Evans broke his arm and the old football players giving touchline advice. When he returns home he is afraid that he might have to join that bank of 'wishful thinkers'. He continues 'I haven't yet met any of our lads, but Dick Watson went to tea where I had been the week before, and I got nearer to seeing Jack Collings than he will ever realise'. 'Gummy' sends all his best wishes to members in the Forces and many thanks to the Committee in the village and myself who are doing so much for him.

Ron 'Gummy' Naylor

Well, that is all for this month. Thank you for your letters. To you all, as always, Good luck and God speed.
Yours very sincerely
F.C. Barrett.

6 Church Lane,
Girton.
July 1945

Dear

For several weeks now I have been worrying and wondering how to find time to write to you. I have been fondly imagining what when peace in Europe came it would bring more leisure time to me; on the contrary this first month of peace has found me even more busy than ever before and that I thought impossible!

This has been a strange summer; I seem to have lost touch with it somehow. You know how the season advances in an orderly manner culminating with the hay harvest, with a scent of coumarin in the air and the sound of bees on the wing. It is also the first season for many a year when I have not had time to play cricket on Saturday afternoon; not that I was ever any good at the game, but of all the various and many games I have played cricket has always been my first love. In football, and such games as basketball or tennis, you are playing so hard and fast that you never have time to stop and enjoy the game, it is always when the game is over that full enjoyment comes, but in cricket you have time to think and enjoy it at many periods. There can also be moments of anxiety when standing far out in the deep and the batsman hits the ball high in the air in your direction; the spectators have time to focus their eyes on it and at the same time discuss with their neighbours whether you will hold it or not, or it can be one of drowsy meditation as you lie under the shade of a tree and hear the distant sound of the ball meeting the bat and the decorous clapping of the spectators. But how often have I watched with trepidation as my turn to bat approaches – I am usually last man in wondering if I shall break my duck. As I now travel round the County I pass the various cricket grounds and I can recall the characteristics of almost every game in which I have played. For instance, how well I remember going with our Girton team to Willingham to decide who should be top of the Cambs. Cricket League. Girton won the toss and decided to bat first and if I remember rightly amassed a fine score. Willingham went in to bat and Cecil Cole and Rev Palmer soon had the wickets falling. Finally the last man was summoned to take his stand at the wicket with 53 runs still to get – I can see him yet, a big hefty fellow as brown as a berry, collar and tie removed – that is if he ever wore one – braces much in evidence, and hob-nailed boots; as he walked to the wicket minus pads and gloves and turning his cloth cap so that the peak was at the back I heard him mutter 'I'll soon knock these blankety blank runs off'. On reaching the wicket he disdained the umpires middle and to my surprise he smote the first ball right out of the ground for six and so he continued till Willingham were the undisputed League champions. I wonder if Harry Cranfield, Tom Impey, and Sid Gawthrop can remember this match? It all goes to show that games are never won or lost until the last ball is bowled, or what excitements may turn up at any moment. Our pitch is now in a sorry state. It is quite difficult to find out just where it was on the Rec, but it will be a small matter to put it in working order once more compared to some of the jobs we have to do.

The young lads of the village are not enthusiastic cricketers; Girton never has been a cricketing village. Mr Palmer, when he was Rector, did manage to evoke some interest in the game. Of the many cricketing communities I know invariably the foundation has been laid and maintained by the parson. How often I have been astonished as I have watched the Vicar on Saturday afternoons slaughter an over-pitched ball or bowl a 'wrong-'un' with such absolute single devotion and yet on Sunday, divest of cricket boots and pads, can become the Parish priest and with dignity impart light and consolation.

Here I must stop writing about cricket. I'm sure I could go on for a very long time but you want to know what has been happening in the village, and of the folks at home. Very little has happened outside the usual run of village life. The election is in full swing and as the result will be published long before you receive this letter I must be careful what I say. There are three candidates for Cambridgeshire, Mr Gerald Howard, Conservative; Lieut. L.E. Goodman, Liberal; and Mr A.E. Stubbs, Labour. Mr Stubbs I would say is known locally more so than the other two; he has been associated with Trades Union and Farm workers in Cambs. for many years. All three candidates have addressed meetings on the village green, but I simply haven't had time to go and hear them. Each group is confident of success and that we may expect the best reforms and progress if we vote for them. What I have noticed about this election, – although the last one is a very long time ago – that most people are anxious to understand each Party's point of view, are asking questions, and demanding satisfying answers. I think one could with certainty say that the people are more politically conscious and this point was proved quite definitely in our own village last month when the Village Institute was packed with people anxious to elect their councillor to sit on the R.D.C. Quite recently two vacancies occurred on the Parish Council and there were no less than 8 candidates nominated. Mr Joe Wilderspin and Mr T.W. Bailey were elected to serve until next March, when we hope to return to normal elections. In the Cambridge Borough there is a straight fight between the retiring member Lieut. Commander R.L. Tuffnell, Conservative, and Major A.L. Symonds, Labour; many of my friends in both parties believe that history will be made in that this will be the first time Cambridge has returned a Labour M.P. The Homecoming and Entertainment Committees continue their good works in organising concerts, whist-drives and dances. There is a close harmony between the two committees, and they are now preparing for a mammoth fete which is to be held on the Recreation Ground on August Bank Holiday Monday; the proceeds from this function are to be divided between the two organisations and it is hoped that it will be bigger, better, and brighter than last year. The Chairman and the Secretary, Messrs. Millar and Dixon respectively, recently resigned from the Homecoming Fund Association, and Mr Joe Wilderspin and Mr T.W. Bailey have succeeded them. One of their first duties they had to do was to officiate at a full committee meeting to consider the draft rules of the Association and define what exactly was meant by certain phrases. Those of you who have seen the rules will realise that of the 12 clauses 10 are devoted to organisation and 2 to the distribution of the fund. As these 2 clauses only affect you, I will tell you about them, Rule (2) states that 'The object of the Association shall be to raise a fund of money by subscription, entertainment, or from which to make a monetary gift upon the homecoming to every member of H.M. Forces, and to every person conscripted to Mine work NORMALLY resident in Girton'. Many people wanted to know what was meant by 'normally' resident in Girton. It has been decided that 'normally' resident in Girton means that a person who will be eligible to receive benefit from the fund had to reside in Girton on the 3rd Sept, 1939. It was also decided that any such resident would be eligible for benefit if she or he joined H.M. Forces at any time after Sept. 3rd, 1939, and the cessation of hostilities with Japan. Rule (8) states 'The committee shall determine from time to time the manner in which effect shall be given to the principle of an equal distribution to all recipients of the fund.' This rule was fully upheld. It was also agreed that no payments would be paid to returning personnel until 3 months after hostilities with Japan, as it was hoped that subscribers to the fund would give thanksgiving donations after that event.

The village Education Society held an exhibition in the W.I. Hall, June 4th–6th inclusive, under the general heading of 'The Primary School' The purpose of the exhibition was to arouse local interest in the great and far-reaching 1944 Education Act, which may well prove to be one of the greatest social reforms of all time, and to show that the work of the ideal Primary School would be based on activity and experience rather than by facts to be stored and knowledge to be gained. With this idea in mind the exhibition demonstrated that one of the first essentials required by the 3–11 year olds is plenty of space both indoors and out. In general section photographs were displayed showing ideal sites of schools, classroom, equipment, apparatus, etc., from Great Britain, America, Russia, the Dominions, and the Colonies; separate sections were devoted to Art, Needlework, Handwork and Physical Education. These sections were most interesting, and showed what excellent work could be done with correct material and apparatus suitable for the various age groups. It was a revelation to stand by any one of these sections for a few moments and hear the remarks of parents as they commented on the high standard of work attained under such conditions. I was particularly interested in this exhibition for I have had the opportunity of visiting and working in Village Colleges in our own county and the new schools of the Isle of Ely, and have seen the methods and ideas advocated by the village Education Society in operation; these ideas are not for Utopia, but are now

The W.I. Hall

available for our children if only we ourselves make the efforts to demand them; in fact we have already been granted the facilities for a Nursery Class in Girton and Mr Garner tells me that Apparatus and furniture is available for the under fives. The Education Society is to be congratulated on a fine piece of work, and we hope they will continue to educate and show us what is available for our children, and we on our own part must put forward every effort to attain it.

And now for news in brief: The N.L. regrets to say that Mr L. Burgess of 47 Thornton Road, is reported missing in Italy. We hope that by the time this letter is printed we shall have received re-assuring news as to his safety. Tom Impey and A.R. Holt have met in India. I have since heard that Mr Holt has been ill. I hope by now he is well again. Claude Kidman has been ill with malaria but has now recovered. It was nice to meet several of our village lads home on leave from various parts of the world. The first one I met was Stan (Diddley) Hankin home from the Middle East. Stan has been working with the War Graves Commission, and he told me he had met Sid Gawthrop and a lad from Oakington while out there. He is delighted to be home but still hasn't got his bearings, the children have all grown up and it takes him quite a while to find out who they are. He is hoping to get a posting close to home. To you all he sends greetings and good wishes. Jack Collings home after 18 months in the Pacific also came to see me; he is fit and well and sends greetings to all of you. Roy 'Gummy' Naylor is reported to have landed in England from the Pacific, we are all looking forward to seeing him home again. 'Frank', another welcome visitor from Germany came to see me; he was a member of the Searchlight Unit which was stationed on the Rec for 2 years. We got to know him so well that we considered him a village lad. He was always known as 'Frank' and it was only quite recently I discovered that his name was William Franklin. He sends best wishes and kind regards to all his friends in the Forces. Tom and Dick Evans are expected home in time for the marriage of their sister Joyce, this weekend. Betty Farrow is also being married this weekend to Charles Weekes, R.A.F.; the N.L. wishes them every Happiness.

And now for the letters: I have received quite a number of interesting letters during the past month or so, and I regret that space does not allow me to quote fully from them all – I should like to say how much I appreciate all your kind remarks and good wishes. John Chapman wrote to say that he has arrived safely in India and is on the look-out for any Girton lads. A newcomer to our village, Jim Berry, whose home is in Pepys Way, and now serving with the R.A.F. Signals in Ceylon sends greetings and best wishes to all. During the short time he spent in Girton before going abroad he learnt to love the village and looks forward to joining the village community when he returns home. We shall be delighted to greet you Jim. A letter from Sid Gawthrop tells me that he has been to Greece, then back to central Italy then on to Cairo, he has been able to have a game or two of cricket, but instead of being the fine batsman as he

Girton Village Cricket Team

was at home has turned bowler and in a recent match took 5 wickets for 16 runs. Sid expresses his gratitude to all at home for the joy and pleasure that he has had through feeling that he has not been forgotten; he hopes to be demobbed early in the new year and looks forward to batting for the village next season. A long and interesting letter from Les Impey tells me that he has been to Florence, seen the Leaning Tower of Pisa, and many other sights in Italy. He is delighted that the war in Europe is over hopes for an early capitulation of Japan. He asks me to let brother Tom and Len Hales know that he will have 'a pint ready for them in the George when they come home' – I am not sure if this is the pint he promised some time ago, or another one, so I think, Les, you had better order, to be on the safe side at least 2 pints. I was also very pleased to receive a letter from Ron Cole, back in Malta after being stationed in Italy. Ron I did not receive your previous letter so it must have been lost as you suggested. Ernest Wilson also wrote me from Florence he like Les Impey was impressed by the fine city; thank you very much indeed for your good wishes and I do hope it wont be long before we see you again, and in the meantime I hope you will be able to meet some of the other Girtonians who are in that area. H.L. Rooke of Pepys Way, who has been $3\frac{1}{2}$ years in the Middle East hopes to come home a civilian in August, in his letter to me, and again I would like to say how much I appreciate them, he expresses the hope that he will be able to join in the activities of the village on his return. Well, Mr Rooke, we await you almost with open arms, for we have lots to do. Finally I must apologise to Dick Evans, he wrote to me in May and by an oversight I did not answer his letter last month. Dick, you are now a real veteran of the line; you seem to have travelled the war-fronts with a vengeance – I am looking forward to seeing you when you come home on leave, and as you say we will have a grand chat about all your doings. In each letter I have received they all conclude with 'Through the N.L. will you please kindly convey my good wishes to all my friends at home and abroad'.

Dick Evans, R.A.

May I therefore take this opportunity of adding my own and passing on the many good wishes from our serving men to you all.

There will be no N.L. for August, but hope to give you more news in the September letter. May I once again send good wishes and as always, good luck, and God speed.
Yours sincerely,
F.C. Barrett.

[There was no letter for August 1945]

6 Church Lane,
Girton.
September 1945

Dear

Tonight as I sit down to write this last N.L., it occurred to me that it is exactly six years ago to the day that the Second World War started. Many will say that it was but a continuation of the last war and the interim period was but a breathing space. That may be, but the history books will record it as the official day. We who have lived through those past six years will recall each passing phase, first the phoney war, the collapse of France, the period when we were alone and the final period when we gained the ascendancy and complete victory over the enemy as something very personal and intimate.

How well I recall that Sunday six years ago. It was a lovely September day, we had been warned that the then Prime Minister, Mr Neville Chamberlain had something important to say. At 11 o'clock the Church bells had just ceased ringing when we were told over the radio, in a voice filled with emotion 'That we should be fighting against evil things'. That same day we heard the wailing of the siren, due as we found out later, to a mistake on someone's part. The next few days were filled with intense activity, building air raid shelters, filling sand bags, and drinking beer in order to quench our thirst, for those were very hot days. While we worked we had half an eye skywards lest the enemy send his bombers to destroy our very existence. This phase passed and in its place came a period in which 'Business as Usual', was the order of the day. It was this same period when we promised to 'Hang out the Washing on the Siegfrid Line'. Quietly there passed from the village first one and then another to join the Forces, some went to France and others trained in England. Those who stayed at home quickly became Wardens, First-Aid men, Firemen, Red Cross Nurses or Special Police. So keen were we in those days that we informed our fellow members, almost with bated breath, that a yellow or a purple was in operation.

Then came the fall of France. A terrifying and awful happening. In our hearts we feared the worst for ourselves and our families, but the blazing sunshine, it always seemed that the sun shone when dreadful things happened, in fact we called it Hitler weather. We steeled ourselves and put on a brave face.

How well we all recall Mr Eden's broadcast, the first L.D.V.s walking round the Parish looking for possible parachutists and in the morning going to work very red eyed. Serious as were those days we still were able to laugh at ourselves, especially when we heard that in a nearby village the L.D.V.s paraded without arms – none were available – but after hearing from the village constable that he would not proceed against anyone possessing a gun without licence no one was surprised when at the next parade almost every man turned up with a double barrel sporting gun!

Immediately after this came a period of intense activity by day and many sirens by night. Can you recall them? Wardens cycling round the Village blowing whistles, the A.F.S. without adequate hose or ladders. The Parish Council provided the First-Aid post, with bandages and dressings; each night we carted fresh water into Mr Searle's tin hut and waited for the nightly symphony. The times we started up our ancient ambulance, a very temperamental creature at the best of times, and how we waited for the bombs to drop. Night after night we watched flashes from falling bombs and heard the distant thud as they hit the ground; this spectacle was enhanced by slow weaving searchlights and the staccato of the Ack Ack guns. All this was bearable during the summer months, but during the winters of 1940–1–2 there were some severe and prolonged frosts, and on one occasion when I went to do my spell of First-Aid duty I found the water in the kettles and hot water bottles frozen solid, and on another occasion when two lady members of the party had to dig their way out in the morning through a deep snow drift.

Then there were those combined exercises with the Home Guard and the Wardens, all night affairs. People called Umpires, I never discovered why, always seemed to be tying labels on victims and lighting thunder flashes, or else conspicuously displaying themselves to the enemy at the critical moment when the defenders were on the point of annihilating them! Still, behind the light-hearted banter there was a real endeavour to be prepared and efficient. Had Girton been blitzed or invaded we should have found amongst us a band of people able to rise to the occasion, this surely was proved by the high commendations received from time to time by the First-Aid Party and the winning by the Home Guard of the Battle Shield in open competition with all Battle Platoons in the Isle of Ely,

Cambridgeshire and Norfolk. All this work was in addition to the heavy strain of daily life, blackout, digging for victory, etc., Many were the people who kept going when normally they would have given in because they felt that to slacken would mean the loss of all that was dear to them.

Early in the war there was formed, with representatives from every organisation in the village, a new body known as the Entertainment Committee. It was this committee's job to raise funds, by means of dances, whist drives, concerts, donations, etc., in order that they could send on behalf of the village small presents to our serving men and women, never with the idea of augmenting their pay, but rather that those who were far from home would not feel forgotten and at the same time express our gratitude for all you were doing. The Committee's functions were well supported and I think I am right in saying that they have raised £1,000 during the war. In addition to working on behalf of the serving men and women they also made themselves responsible for the welfare of Village and evacuated children by giving a party at Xmas and sports on Whit Monday.

During this period Girton men and women were steadily being called up, trained and then drafted to all parts of the Globe. Some were rushed to the Near East to stop Rommel's march into Egypt and some – we still don't know why or how – were taken prisoner by the Japanese. Cambridge and district have had to bear a heavy burden for the 1st and 2nd Battalions of the Cambridgeshires were lost in that unfortunate campaign. Now with the war over tension is again rising. People are wondering and hoping that their loved ones are alive and well. Thus awful strain has been further aggravated by the fact that a postcard which took a year to reach this country was the only communication, and added to this were tales of inhuman treatment, starvation, disease to which the prisoners were subjected. Now the tension is almost unbearable waiting, it has always been waiting, to hear if they are alive and well and how long it will be before they return home.

As the war advanced, the sky filled with more and more bombers. Day and night we were subjected to the roar of their engines, and we knew now that victory could not long be delayed and we marvelled how the enemy could stand such poundings. Then came invasion, V.E. days, and a few weeks later came atomic bombs, and V.J. days, and peace.

Dare we say Peace – it is already an uneasy peace, let us hope that this is but the birth pangs and that as mankind faces what might be its last chance to redeem itself there will be forged a lasting end endurable peace.

In such a short review of our village during the war many things have unavoidably been left out for want of space, but I do hope that at a later date this will be rectified. While trying to collect some details of Girton's history for the recent exhibition given by the Youth Centre I was amazed how little was known about the past. I was told on all sides that Girton had no history, but I refuse to believe that a village which had an existence before Domesday Book was compiled has no history, rather I think that no-one ever bothered to write about the present, to them it was unimportant. The same is true today, we are living in and making history, so let us write an account of it. I guarantee that it will make most interesting reading in 25 years time, to say nothing of how it will be appreciated in 100 or 200 years' time.

I would love to have had the opportunity of reading what Girton did during the battles between Cromwell and the King's men, and who supported which, or later what happened in the Napoleonic wars. But that is not to be for there is no record. Now, when you come home, what about helping to compile a record of Girton 1939–45?

And now to what has been happening in the Village since I last wrote. The grain harvest has ripened and in most cases is safely gathered in leaving the desolate stubble, and the promise of winter. On the allotments, bent backs are to be seen as potatoes are dug ready for winter store, and on either side of the hedgerows young and old are picking blackberries aided by walking sticks and step ladders.

The weather has not been very kind. Since the last days of July it has been cloudy and cool and a lot of rain has fallen for this time of year.

The combined committees of the Entertainment and Homecoming Fund arranged a grand fete on August Bank Holiday, but it was marred by an intermittent thunderstorm which kept many people away. The fete was similar in scope to the one which was held last year with its sideshows, model railway, treasure hunt, bowling for the pig, etc., etc. Many friends rallied round and helped to make it a success in spite of the weather and a profit of £106 was made. This is to be divided equally between the two organisations. The Homecoming Fund has been very busy organising concerts, dances, and whist drives, and their cash at the Bank stood at £655 at the end of July.

Of the V.J. days and festivities I can tell you only what I have heard, for I was tramping amongst the Scottish mountains and did not know about V.J. until it was V.J.+1. I understand the Parish Council called a meeting and a tea was quickly organised for the children, cakes, buns and money poured in, and a good feed was had by all. After the tea sports were held on the Recreation Ground, and a large bonfire was lit. Later dancing was held in the Women's Institute for parents and friends and by all accounts it was most enjoyable.

Next Saturday it is proposed to conclude the celebrations by giving all the inhabitants of 65 years and over a high tea.

It is with deep regret that I tell you that it has now been established that Mr L. Burgess lost his life in Italy. He will be remembered not only as an Art Master at the Central School, Cambridge, but as a charming and likeable helper with the Girton Boys' Club, and for a short time a member of the First-Aid Party. To Mrs Burgess, who must have suffered intensely while awaiting definite news, the N.L. extends its sincere sympathy.

I meant to have told you some time ago that a small Committee selected from the Reconstruction Committee met the County General Purposes Committee in the Shirehall and placed before them the urgent need for a new Junior School, and the necessity of a Community Centre in our village. We were received kindly and G.P.C. were sympathetic and readily appreciated our problem. They promised to survey the matter, and discuss with the diocesan authorities the difficulties which would arise through Girton possessing an Endowed School. They were most interested in our plans for a Community Centre and promised to give the matter urgent consideration so that we may obtain our Centre at the earliest possible opportunity.

It has been great fun meeting so many Girtonians home on leave during the past few weeks. At one period I saw Tom, Dick and Will Evans, Roy Naylor, Ron Lipscombe, Cliff Hankin and Jack Collings all home together. Since then Ron Cole has returned from journeying between Malta, Italy and France, and I understand that E.J. Stearn is home from the Middle East. It was a great pleasure to receive a visit from Les Impey, he looks fit and well after his service in Italy. He told me of his interesting journeys since war ended and I enquired if he has had that pint he promised his brother and Len Hales, put on the shelf. He assured me that it is placed on the top shelf and there it will remain pending their arrival to do it justice.

This month I have received two letters, one from my faithful correspondent J. Chapman now in India. John is still on the lookout for any Girton lads, so far he has only met a lad from Ross St, and another from Bourn. The three meet each week and great is their disappointment if one of them has not received a copy of the Cambs. Weekly News.

I was delighted to receive a letter from Mr A.R. Holt, but I was sorry to hear that be has been ill for so long. When he wrote he was about to be discharged from hospital and was going to a convalescent camp. In his letter be gave a vivid description of his meeting with Tom Impey in the heart of Burma, and the enjoyable time they spent together. Of the scenery in Burma he says 'It is really wonderful, Kanchenjunga we can see on a clear day towering up in the sky like a fairy castle. We overlook a big tea plantation and one gets a feeling of tremendous space.' Mr Holt continues 'Burma was better than expected, but everything is very primitive, all kinds of flying pests, crawling reptiles; but apart from the heat and mosquitoes it's not too bad!' You will have noticed in my opening sentence I said this would be my last N.L. This I am afraid is so, as both Miss Wallis and myself find that with the coming of peace we shall be caught up in a vast amount of extra work, and as many of you are or will be very soon returning to 'Civvy Street' we think it an opportune moment to cease publication.

I shall always recall with pleasure the many friends I have made, the many interesting letters I have received, and I only hope that you on your part feel that the N.L. was, if not always particularly newsy, worthwhile. Although the N.L. will end, I shall be delighted to hear from you.

Miss Wallis and I salute you all, and I await the pleasure of meeting you when you return to Girton.

To you all may I send again my best wishes and, as always, Good luck and God speed.

Yours very sincerely,

F.C. Barrett.

Letters Received in Reply

Freddie Barrett received a total of 107 letters from 44 Girton service men and women during the life of the Newsletters, from March 1943 to September 1945.

Barber, R.H. (L.A.C. 1242229)
29 June 1943, from 7(C) O.T.U. Detachment R.A.F., Co Antrim, N Ireland.

Berry, J.G. (Signalman 14646742)
31 May 1945, from 230 Independent Coy, Air Formation Signals, c/o R.A.F. Ceylon.

Burrows, R.S. (AC/2 2207409 R.A.F.)
18 Dec 1943, from 4822 Flight A.C.S. R.A.F. Station, Seighford, Stafford.

Chapman, J. (Gnr 5836749, R.A.)
24 Oct 1943, from 420 Hy A.A. Bty R.A., C.P.O. Lincoln.
9 Nov 1943, from 420/140 Hy A.A. Regt R.A. No 1 Section A Troop, Leigh on Sea, Essex.
24 Dec 1943, from 420 Hy A.A. Bty R.A. Leicester.
15 Feb 1944, from 420 Hy A.A. Bty R.A. 1 Section A Troop, Enderby, Leicester.
Apr 1944 [envelope], from 420 Hy A.A. Bty R.A. 1 Section A Troop, Rockingham Camp, Nr Corby, Northants.
30 Apr 1944, from 420 Hy A.A. Bty R.A. 1 Section A Troop, New Milton, Hampshire.
22 July 1944, from 420 Hy A.A. Bty R.A. 1 Section A Troop, Lydd, Kent.
31 Aug 1944, from No 5 Platoon B Coy, 291/87 L.A.A. Regt R.A., Topsham Barracks, Exeter, Devon.
18 Oct 1944, from 420/140 Hy A.A. Bty R.A. 1 Section A Troop, Woodbridge, Suffolk.
14 Jan 1945, from No 5 Platoon B Coy, 291/87 L.A.A. Regt R.A., Topsham Barracks, Exeter, Devon.
24 Jan 1945, from Welch Regt 5 Platoon B Coy 291/87 L.A.A. Regt R.A., Topsham Barracks, Exeter Devon.
1 Mar 1945, from 5 Platoon, B Coy E Troop 291/87 L.A.A. Regt R.A., Topsham Barracks, Devon.
17 June 1945, from Welch Regt H.Q. Co, H.Q. B.B.S.T.E. India Command.
12 July 1945, from Welch Regt A Coy 2 Wing B.B.S.T.E., India Command.
Spring 1945, from R.P.F.R.H.Z. India Command.
Aug 1945, from L/Cpl Welch Regt D Coy 2 Wing B.B.S.T.E. India Command.

Chapman, H.J. (Dvr. T/227531 R.A.S.C.)
13 May 1945, from C Coy, 1 Div 7 Con Depot C.M.F.
23 Jan 1944?, from A Platoon, 328 Div Troops Coy, R.A.S.C. C.M.F. Italy.

Cole, R.N. (A/B. C/J.X544034 R.N.)
9 July 1943, from S.B1/1323 H.M.S. Ganges, Mess 13, Rodney Div Shotley, Ipswich.
21 June 1944?, from Mess 172 c/o C.F.B. Malta.

Collings, J. (A.Me. F.X101678 R.N.)
1 Jan 1944, from c/o S.B.N.O. U.S. Naval Air Station, Brunswick, Maine, U.S.A.
16 July 1944, from H.M.S. Bambara c/o Bristol Fleet Mail.
Christmas 1944, from Mess 46 H.M.S. Illustrious, c/o G.P.O.

London. (Illustrious Christmas card)
19 Mar 1945, from Mess 46 H.M.S. Illustrious, c/o G.P.O. London.
Cranfield, A.P. (P/L.X. 24687 R.N.)
17 Nov 19??, from 114 Mess H.M.S. Howe, c/o G.P.O. London.
3 Sept 1943, from 114 Mess H.M.S. Howe, c/o G.P.O. London.
22 Mar 1944?, from 114 Mess H.M.S. Howe, c/o G.P.O. London.
Cranfield, H.R. (Cpl 736556)
27 July 1943, from 13 Field Dressing Station, Sittingbourne, Kent.
17 July 1944, from 13 Field Dressing Station, B.L.A.
Dixon, S.K. (F/Lt. R.A.F.)
30 Mar 1944, from 204 Officers' Mess.
Dupont, F. (L.A.C. 1428268 R.A.F.)
4 Feb 1944, from Station Sick Quarters, Waterbeach, Cambs.
Durham, W. (Sgt. 2045245 R.A.)
5 Sept 1944 [envelope], from A Troop, 333 Searchlight Bty, R.A. Molash, Nr Canterbury, Kent.
Ellis, R.B.F. (Pte. 144110821 Beds & Herts Regt)
6 Jun 1943 [envelope], from 6th Btn Beds & Herts C Company, Caterham, Surrey.
8 Dec 1943, from 6th Btn Beds & Herts, Demo Platoon Att 54th Div.
14 Feb 1944, from 6th Beds & Herts, C Coy, Beckenham, Kent.
4 Jan 1945, from 1st Bn Herefordshire Regt A Coy 7 Pln, B.L.A.
2 May 19??, from 6th Bn Bedfordshire & Hertfordshire Regt C Coy, Beckenham, Kent.
Engledow, M. (W.L.A.)
Undated card bearing Women's Land Army crest thanking Freddie Barrett for Newsletter.

Evans, A. (Pte. 14411127 Beds & Herts Regt)
22 May 1944 [envelope], from Beds & Herts Regt Att D Coy, 20th Royal Fusiliers, Indian Command.
23 Nov 1944, from 4M Coy 1st Northants S.E.A.C.
6 Aug 1945, from 4M Coy 1st Northants, S.E.A.C.
Evans, R. (Gnr. 14713130 R.A.)
22 Dec 1944, from 85 Bty, 11 Medium Regt R.A., D Troop, B.L.A.
20 May 1945, from 85 Bty, B Troop 11 Medium Regt R.A., B.L.A.
12 Dec 1944, from 85 Bty, 11 Medium Regt R.A., B Troop, B.L.A.
14 Dec 1944 (Christmas card).
Evans, T. (Bevin Boy)
16 Dec 1944, from Mansfield, Notts.
Gawthrop, S. (Trooper 5834630 R.A.C.)
25 May 1944, from 142 Regt Royal Armoured Corps B Squadron C.M.F., Italy.
23 Jun 1945, from Kings Dragoon Guards H.Q. Sqn M.E.F.
Griffiths, C.B. (Pte. 7406039)
3 Dec 1943, from 77 I.S.S. c/o No 6 Advance Base, Post Office, India Command.
10 Oct 1944, from T.E.C. 77 I.S.S.C.D. S.E.A.C.
Xmas 1944, from S.E.A.C., India.
1 Apr 1945, from B.M.H. Shillong S.E.A.C.
Hales, L.M. (Cpl Y139008 R.A.S.C.)
18 Sept 1943, from R.A.S.C. 553 Tank Transport Coy, India Command.
6 July 1944, from L/Cpl T/139008 C Platoon, 553 Tank Transport Coy, R.A.S.C. India Command.
9 Mar 1945, from C Platoon, 553 Coy R.A.S.C. (Tank Transport) S.E.A.C.

Hancock, K. (Pte. 14055163)
14 Dec 1945, from Paschendaele Hut, T.Coy 31 T.C., Blenheim Camp, Bury St Edmunds, Suffolk.

Hankin, C.W. (Dvr. 14499632 R.A.S.C.)
1 Dec 1943 [envelope], from R.A.S.C. Barry, Glam, S Wales.
9 Dec 1944, from Ward 4, General Hospital, Halifax.

Hind, J. (Cpl 1615037 R.A.F.)
4 Jan 1944, from 12S of T.T. R.A.F. India.

Holt, A.R. (Cpl 1871706)
6 Aug 1945, from C.M.H. Lebong, Darjeeling, India Command.

Huddlestone, G. (?)
15 Jan 1944, from Canadian Y.M.C.A.

Impey, L.G. (Cpl 7630284)
10 Sept 1943, from No 1 Base, Ammunitions Depot, R.A.O.C., B.N.A.F.
16 Aug 1944, from No 1 O.A.C. R.A.O.C., Att 14 B.A.D. C.M.F.
9 Dec 1944, from No 1 O.A.C. R.A.O.C., Att 14 B.A.D. C.M.F.
15 Jan 1945, from No 1 O.A.C. R.A.O.C., Att 14 B.A.D. C.M.F.
1 June 1945, from 543 O.A.C. R.A.O.C., C.M.F.
3 Aug 1945, from 543 O.A.C. R.A.O.C., 501 Bfd C.M.F.

Impey, T.C. (S/Sgt. 1896999)
5 May 1944, from C-in-C's (E2AIR) Branch, G.H.Q. India Command, New Delhi.
5 Feb 1945, from c/o D.C.R.E. 145 Works (Ind) S.E.P.C. [?S.E.A.C.]

Jaggard, R.J. (L.A.C. 1218238 R.A.F.)
30 Sept 1944, from Permanent Staff 25, F.T.C. R.A.F., M.E.F.

Kidman, C. (A.C. 1521571 R.A.F.)
11 Aug 1943, from R.A.F. India Command.
4 June 1944, from H.Q. Air Command South East Asia.
22 Jan 1945, from Ambala, R.A.F. India.

Lipscombe, R. (A/B P/TX. 395296 R.N.)
7 Jan 19??, from c/o Dems office, Colombo, Ceylon.

Macalister, J. (Sgt. W1076861 A.T.S.)
13 Dec 1944, no address.

Naylor, R. (Marine CH/X 112426 R.N.)
18 Apr 1943 [envelope], from W Gang, 258 Squad, c/o Royal Marine Depot, Deal, Kent.
12 Aug 1943, from G Coy B12 K.B. Chatham, Kent.
25 Feb 1944, from H.M.S. Nelson.
6 Sept 1944, from 558 Flotilla R.M., c/o G.P.O. London.
15 Dec 1944, from 558 Flotilla R.M.
9 Feb 1945, from 558 Flotilla R.M.
22 Apr 1945, from 558 Flotilla.

Parfitt, K.M. (Pte. W/139443)
18 Feb 1944, from 2 Section, A Troop, 542(M) Hy A.A. Bty R.A., Mount Road, Gorton, Manchester.
17 Apr 1944, from 2 Section, A Troop, 542(M) Hy A.A. Bty R.A., Through-end-Field Mauldeth Road Chorlton-cum-Hardy, Manchester.
6 Aug 1944, from 542 Bty R.A., Shoreham, Sussex. 27 Dec 1944, from A Troop, 542 Bty R.A.
5 Feb 1945, from B 4th A Troop 542 Bty R.A., Gt Wakering, Essex.

Pauley, T. (Pte. 5833854 R.A.S.C.)
10 Aug 1943, from T.A. 5/R.W.K., No 1 E.C.T.C., M.E.F.
25 Nov 1943, from 5/R W.K. C Coy No 1 Btn No 1 I.T.D., M.E.F.
30 Jan 1944, from 5/R W.K. No 1 E.C.T.C., M.E.F.
23 Mar 1944, from A.C.C. 35 D.I.D. R.A.S.C., M.E.F.

Purkiss, R.J. (Sgt. 2614403 Grenadier Guards)
8 May 1944, from No 2 Coy 3rd Btn Grenadier Guards C.M.F.

Purkiss, W.J. (Cpl 622080 R.A.F.)
29 Apr 1945, from R.A.F., Nassau, Bahamas.

Riley, J.V. (Bdr. 937880 R.A.)
29 Sept 1944, from 472/99 Fld Rgt R.A. S.E.A.C.

Rooke, H.L. (S/Sgt. 7358584)
10 June 1944, from C.R.E. Works 28 P.A.I.E. Force, Iraq.
12 June 1944, from R.E. 335 R.E. Works Section P.A.I. Force.
4 July 1945, from 265 R.E. Works Section 59 C.R.E. (Works), M.E.F.

Scott, R. (L/Cpl T/238756 R.A.S.C.)
26 Mar 1945, from B Platoon, 88 Coy R.A.S.C. (M.A.C.), C.M.F.

Stearn, E.J. (S/Sgt. 2131254 R.E.)
13 July 1943, from R.E. C.E. Aerodromes, G.H.Q., M.E.F.
21 Jan 1944, from Q.M.S. R.E. 34 C.R.E. Aerodrome, M.E.F.
22 Nov 1944 [envelope], from W.O. II R.E. H.Q. 34 C.R.E. (Works) A.E. R.O.D.R., M.E.F.

Wakelin, J. (Lieut. R.A.S.C.)
27 Dec 1943, from 54 B.S.D. Melmerby Hall, Melmerby, Penrith, Cumberland.
13 Nov 1944 [envelope], from 27 H.Q. C.R.A.S.C. (Sup Units), B.L.A.

Wilson, E.C. (Dvr T/196 R.A.S.C.)
29 May 1945, from No 1 British I.C.R.U., D Coy, R.A.S.C., C.M.F.

Young, G. (AC/2 3001202 R.A.F.)
11 Nov 1943, from Hut X19, B Squadron, 2 Wing R.A.F. Weeton, Nr Preston, Lancs.

The War Memorial, Girton with (inset) the names of those who died in the Second War

Abbreviations

Those marked '*Unknown*' are presumably local or temporary units.

4M Coy	4 Mules Company	C.M.H.	Commonwealth Military Hospital
A.A.	Anti-Aircraft	C.O.	Commanding Officer
A.C.	Air Corps	C.R.A.S.C.	Commander Royal Army Service Corps
A.C.C.	Army Catering Corps		
A.C.S.	Advanced Communication System	C.R.E.	Command Royal Engineers
A.D.	Ammunition Depot	Cambs	Cambridgeshire
A.E.	Aerodrome	Capt.	Captain
A.F.S.	Auxiliary Fire Service	Coy	Company
A.Me.	Artificer Mechanic	Cpl	Corporal
A.O.C.	Air Officer Commanding	D.C.R.E.	Deputy Command Royal Engineers
A.R.P.	Air Raid Precautions	D.E.M.S.	Defensively equipped merchant ships
A.T.S.	Auxiliary Territorial Service	D.I.D.	Detailed Issue Depot
A/B	Able Seaman (Able-bodied Seaman)	D.S.O.	Distinguished Service Order
AC/2	Aircraftman/2	Demob.	Demobilization of troops after end of war
Ack Ack	Anti-Aircraft		
Att.	Attached [to]	Dvr	Driver
B.A.D	Base Ammunition Depot	E.C.T.C.	*Unknown*
		E2AIR	E2 Aerodrome
B.A.D.	Base Ammunition Depot	Esq.	Esquire
B.B.C.	British Broadcasting Company	F.A.N.Y.	First Aid Nursing Yeomanry
B.B.S.T.E.	*Unknown*	F.C.B.	Freddie Barrett
B.C.	British Columbia	F.L.S.	Fellow of the Linnean Society
B.L.A.	British Liberation Army	F.R.H.S.	Fellow of the Royal Horticultural Society
B.M.H.	British Military Hospital	F.T.C.	Flying Training Command
B.N.A.F.	British North Africa Force	G.H.Q.	General Headquarters
B.S.D.	Base Service Depot	G.P.C.	General Purposes Committee
Btn	Battalion	G.T.C.	Girls' Training Corps
Bty	Battery	Gen.	General
C-in-C	Commander in Chief	Gnr	Gunner
C.E.	Construction Engineer	H.G.	Home Guard
C.E.M.A.	Council for Economic Mutual Assistance	H.M.	His Majesty; His Majesty's
C.F.B.	Central Fuelling Base	H.M.S.	His Majesty's Ship
C.M.F.	Central Mediterranean Force; Commonwealth Military Forces	H.Q.	Headquarters
		Hy A.A.	Heavy anti-aircraft